GUANTÁNAMO

GUANTÁNAMO

WHY THE ILLEGAL US BASE
SHOULD BE RETURNED TO CUBA

FIDEL CASTRO

Olga Miranda
Roger Ricardo

Ocean Press
Melbourne ▪ New York ▪ London
www.oceanbooks.com.au

ISBN 978-0-9804292-5-1
Library of Congress Catalog Card Number 2010936654

First Printed 2011
Printed in the USA

PUBLISHED BY OCEAN PRESS

Australia: PO Box 1015, North Melbourne, Vic 3051, Australia

USA: 511 Ave of the Americas, #96, New York,
          NY 10011-8436, USA
E-mail: info@oceanbooks.com.au

OCEAN PRESS TRADE DISTRIBUTORS

United States: **Consortium Book Sales and Distribution**
          Tel: 1-800-283-3572 www.cbsd.com

Canada: **Publishers Group Canada**
          Tel: 1-800-663 5714 customerservice@raincoast.com

Australia and New Zealand: **Palgrave Macmillan**
          E-mail: customer.service@macmillan.com.au

UK and Europe: **Turnaround Publisher Services**
          E-mail: orders@turnaround-uk.com

Cuba and Latin America: **Ocean Sur**
          E-mail: info@oceansur.com

www.oceanbooks.com.au
info@oceanbooks.com.au

Contents

Publisher's Note

The military base established by the United States over a century ago at Guantánamo Bay, Cuba, is the oldest US military base outside of the United States. It is also the only foreign military base maintained against the wishes of the government of the host country and the only US military base to be situated in a socialist country. Moreover, it is the only US military base with an indefinite lease.

The 29-kilometer land border of the base is sometimes referred to as the "cactus curtain" because of the large species of cactus planted by the United States around it. The base is located in what has been described as one of the world's great natural harbors, surrounded by a US-placed minefield said to be the largest in the Western world. The main gate to the 45-square-mile area of the base has been closed for almost five decades, since the United States severed all diplomatic and economic ties with Cuba.

When and how will this historical affront to a sovereign nation be resolved? When will the United States return this territory to Cuba? In recent years, there has been much discussion and debate about the closure of the prison on the US naval base at Guantánamo, but barely a voice is heard calling for the full closure of the base and the return of this territory to Cuba. The statement by Nobel Prize winners and others included as the foreword to this volume deserves to be echoed loudly within the international community. There is a simple and just solution to this situation:

The United States can withdraw its troops and close the base.

It is beyond comprehension why the continued existence of the US base on Cuban soil—indisputably against Cuba's wishes—is not an international scandal.

This brief volume offers an overview of the US naval base at Guantánamo—primarily from a Cuban perspective. This is a voice not often heard, largely because of the information blockade that surrounds the island, a blockade almost as effective as the economic blockade imposed some five decades ago.

Most important here is the recent contribution by Fidel Castro. There is no more authoritative voice of Cuba that could and should be heard on this subject. Together with the documents and chronology that are included, this book is an invaluable resource for anyone interested in understanding the background and ongoing injustice—not to mention the violation of international law—of the US base in Cuba.

Foreword

The United States Must Leave Guantánamo Now!

For over a century the United States has intervened, made war and imposed imperialist treaties against the rights of the Cuban people to sovereignty of their country.

In 1897, as Cuba was nearing victory in its second war of independence from Spain, Theodore Roosevelt urged US President McKinley to intervene. In 1898, the United States declared war against Spain to prevent Cuba from gaining its independence.

In 1901, among other measures imposed to codify control of Cuba, including an allowance that the United States may "intervene militarily at any time," was the equally outrageous edict that Cuba must sell or lease to a foreign state, the United States, "lands necessary for coaling or naval stations at certain specific points." Outrageous because these turned out to be, or were always intended to be, the invasion and annexation of that country's territory by a foreign state.

Guantánamo was such a "specific point." A US naval base was built there with well-known consequences. The poverty of the formerly colonialized country was unashamedly exploited by democratic USA with the annual payment of $2,000 in gold, on the self-righteous premise that it is the moral privilege of a rich power to buy anything, including part of another country's territory. Since 1959 Cuba has not accepted that payment.

The use made in recent years of this stolen sovereign territory is to the shame and disgrace of the United States and the rest of the world, which, intimidated by US power, turns a blind eye to the outrageous prison that has been established in another's country. The horrifyingly inhuman conditions of isolation, deprivation and torture in this medieval-like prison, condemned by Amnesty International and an increasing number of human rights organizations, continue to be perpetrated by the foreign power, the United States, which has no right to be there in the first place.

There are many desecrations of human rights taking place in our world today. Many involve conflicts of great complexity — religious or factional — for which it is immensely difficult to create just solutions.

Guantánamo is the outstanding exception.

The just solution is simple.

All nations, communities and every individual throughout the world who believe that relations between nations must be based on the principle of justice should demand that the United States leaves Guantánamo unconditionally. Now!

Noam Chomsky, Nadine Gordimer, Salim Lamrani,
Rigoberta Menchú and Adolfo Pérez Esquivel
19 July, 2005

CHRONOLOGY

1808 Thomas Jefferson sends General James Wilkinson to Cuba to find out if the Spanish would consider ceding Cuba to the United States. Spain is not interested.

1809-1810 Former President Jefferson writes to his successor, James Madison, in 1809, "I candidly confess that I have ever looked upon Cuba as the most interesting addition that can be made to our system of States." With Cuba and Canada, he says, "we should have such an empire for liberty as she has never surveyed since the creation." But Madison settles on a policy of leaving Cuba to the domination of Spain, a relatively weak country, while guarding against its seizure by any mightier power. In 1810, Madison instructs his minister to Great Britain to tell the British that the United States will not sit idly by if Britain were to try to gain possession of Cuba.

1818 Spain allows Cuban ports to open for international trade. Within two years, over half of Cuba's trade is with the United States.

April 28, 1823 Having acquired East and West Florida from Spain a few years earlier, the United States has expanded to within 90 miles of Cuba. In a letter to Minister to Spain Hugh Nelson, Secretary of State John Quincy Adams describes the likelihood of US "annexation of Cuba" within half a century despite obstacles: "But there are laws of political as well as of physical gravitation; and if an apple severed by the tempest from its native tree cannot choose but fall to the ground, Cuba, forcibly disjoined from its own unnatural connection with Spain, and incapable of self support, can gravitate only towards the North American Union, which by the same law of nature cannot cast her off from its bosom." Cubans call this policy *la fruta madura* (ripe fruit); Washington would wait until the fruit is considered ripe for the picking.

December 2, 1823 In what becomes known as the Monroe Doctrine, President James Monroe stakes out the Western Hemisphere as a US sphere of influence by warning Europe not to interfere in the affairs of any of the American nations that have recently become independent while stating concomitantly that the United States will not interfere in European affairs.

1830s-1870s Cuba's sugar industry becomes the most mechanized in the world. By 1850, sugar provides 83 percent of exports, with 40 percent of that going to the United States, part of the Triangular Trade: sugar to the United States, rum to Africa, slaves to Cuba.

1847 As the Mexican War moves closer toward victory for the United States, proponents of "Manifest Destiny" step up efforts to annex Cuba. Some US citizens conspire with a new secret organization of pro-annexation Cubans, the *Club de La Habana*.

1848 In May, Democrats in the United States nominate for president Senator Lewis Cass, who has publicly advocated the purchase of Cuba. Later in the month, Democratic President James Polk secretly decides to try to buy Cuba, in accordance with official policy of annexation only with the consent of Spain. In July, Secretary of State James Buchanan instructs US Minister to Cuba Romulus Saunders to negotiate the deal, but negotiations fall apart amidst conspiracy and betrayal.

1854 Franklin Pierce wins the 1852 election by a landslide as pro-expansionist candidate. In October, Pierce's ministers to Spain (Pierre Soulé), France (J.Y. Mason) and England (James Buchanan) draw up the Ostend Manifesto recommending that the United States purchase Cuba. This manifesto warns against permitting "Cuba to be Africanized and become a second St. Domingo [referring to the Black republic created by the slave insurrection led by Toussaint], with all its attendant horrors to the white race." If Spain refuses to sell, the ministers claim that "we shall be justified in wresting it from Spain... upon the very same principle that would justify an individual in tearing down the burning house of his neighbor if there were no other means of preventing the flames from destroying his own home."

1857-1861 President James Buchanan tries repeatedly to interest Congress in buying Cuba, but Congress is too bitterly divided over slavery.

October 10, 1868 The Ten Years' War (Cuba's first War of Independence) begins when plantation owner Carlos Manuel de Céspedes, accompanied by 37 other planters, proclaims the independence of Cuba in the *Grito de Yara* issued from his plantation. Céspedes frees and arms his slaves. Two days later the brothers Antonio and José Maceo — free blacks — join the rebel ranks. Some Dominican exiles, including Máximo Gómez, help to train the rebels, using their experience from fighting against Spain on nearby Hispaniola. Ignacio Agramonte leads the revolt in Camagüey until he is killed in battle in 1873.

April 10, 1869 A constituent assembly in Guáimaro prepares the first Constitution of the Republic of Cuba and elects Carlos Manuel de Céspedes as the first president.

September 26, 1872 Colombian Foreign Minister Don Gil Colunje proposes a joint action to all Latin American republics and the United States to achieve Cuban independence and the abolition of slavery. The plan, which would be carried out under the leadership of the United States, would offer to reimburse Spain for the loss of the colony with money raised from all the republics. The Latin American governments agree, but US President Ulysses S. Grant rejects the idea.

1880s   The US government prepares for overseas expansion, wiping out Native American resistance in the West and building an offensive navy. Investment by the United States in Cuba increases rapidly. Of Cuban exports, 83 percent go to the United States, only 6 percent to Spain.

November 1897   Spain's queen regent offers autonomy to Cuba, but both the rebels and Cuban loyalists reject the offer. Meanwhile, in Washington, Navy Assistant Secretary Theodore Roosevelt is urging President William McKinley to intervene.

December 24, 1897   US Undersecretary of War J.C. Breckenridge sends instructions to Lt. General Nelson A. Miles concerning US plans for Cuba, Puerto Rico and the Hawaiian Islands (see Document 1).

January 1898   The United States uses rumors of danger to US citizens in Cuba as the reason for dispatching the *USS Maine* to Havana.

February 15, 1898   The battleship *Maine* blows up in Havana's harbor, killing 260 officers and crew. The United States blames Spain. "Remember the *Maine*" becomes a battle cry as the US "yellow press," spearheaded by William Randolph Hearst's chain, shapes public opinion.

April 10, 1898   Spain, having ordered a unilateral suspension of hostilities, sends a message to Washington offering a deal: the United States would indicate terms of an armistice; Cuba would be granted autonomy; the matter of the *Maine* would be submitted to arbitration.

April 11, 1898   President McKinley sends a message to US Congress asking for authority to intervene militarily in Cuba. The message says, "The only hope of relief and repose from a condition which can no longer be endured is the enforced pacification of Cuba."

April 20, 1898   The US Congress declares that Cuba has the right to be free and independent and authorizes the president to use military force to oust Spain. The Teller Amendment adds that the United States has no "intention to exercise sovereignty, jurisdiction, or control over said Island except for the pacification thereof." McKinley signs this declaration and sends it to Spain with the message that he will carry it out unless Spain responds satisfactorily by April 23.

April 22, 1898 President McKinley declares a blockade of the northern coast of Cuba and its port at Santiago, an act of war according to international law.

April 24, 1898 Responding to the US act of war, Spain declares war.

April 25, 1898 The US Congress formally declares war. In the United States, this is known as the Spanish-American War. In Cuba, it is known as the US intervention in Cuba's War of Independence.

August 12, 1898 Spain and the United States sign a bilateral armistice. Cuba is not represented at the negotiations.

December 10, 1898 Spain and the United States sign the Treaty of Paris [see Document 2]. The United States emerges with control of four new territories: Cuba, Puerto Rico, the Philippines and Guam. Although the treaty officially grants Cuba independence, the US flag — not the Cuban flag — is raised over Havana. The United States installs a military government to pacify Cuba.

January 1, 1899 Spain formally surrenders its jurisdiction in Cuba to US military forces commanded by General John R. Brooke, the first US military governor.

December 23, 1899 General Leonard Wood, veteran of US campaigns against Native Americans, replaces Brooke as military governor.

1900 General Wood calls an election for a Cuban constitutional convention, which meets in November and draws up a constitution modeled upon the US Constitution without specifying the nature of future relations with the United States.

March 2, 1901   To codify control of Cuba, the US Congress adds the Platt Amendment to an Army Appropriations bill [see Document 3]. The amendment provides that Cuba has only a limited right to conduct its own foreign policy and debt policy; the United States may intervene militarily at any time; the Isle of Pines shall be omitted from the boundaries of Cuba until the title to it is adjusted by future treaty; Cuba will sell or lease to the United States "lands necessary for coaling or naval stations at certain specified points to be agreed upon." Since the US government makes it clear that its military occupation will not end until this amendment becomes part of Cuban law, Cuba incorporates the Platt Amendment into its 1901 Constitution.

1901   General Wood supervises what the United States calls a democratic election for national offices, but the franchise excludes Afro-Cubans, women and those with less than $250. Tomás Estrada Palma is elected president.

May 20, 1902   The US military occupation ends as Estrada becomes president.

March 1903   Cuba and the United States ratify a treaty on commercial reciprocity, ensuring US control of Cuban markets.

May 22, 1903   Cuba and the United States sign the "Permanent Treaty" which incorporates the Platt Amendment.

July 2, 1903   To follow up the Platt Amendment provision for selling or leasing coaling and naval bases to the United States, Cuba signs a treaty with the United States agreeing to lease Bahía Honda and Guantánamo. This prepares the way for the construction of a US naval base at Guantánamo, a deep-water port in eastern Cuba. The price of the lease for Guantánamo is set at $2,000 a year in gold. The same year, the administration of President Theodore Roosevelt engineers the separation of

Panama from Colombia and arranges to build the Panama
Canal. On this same day the United States signs a treaty with
Cuba agreeing to relinquish all claim to the Isle of Pines, but the
US Senate refuses to ratify within the stipulated seven months.

March 2, 1904 Cuba and the United States sign a new treaty about
the Isle of Pines, this time with no deadline for ratification [see
Document 6].

1904-1905 President Roosevelt formulates his corollary to the
Monroe Doctrine: since the United States does not allow
European nations to intervene in Latin America, then the
United States has responsibility for preserving order and
protecting life and property in those countries.

August 1906 President Estrada requests US intervention to put
down an insurrection. President Roosevelt sends Secretary
of War William Howard Taft as mediator. Estrada objects to
Taft's proposals and resigns in September. The United States
exercises its Platt Amendment authorization to intervene and
sends in US Marines for a second military occupation.

September 29, 1906 The US Secretary of War heads a provisional
government of Cuba.

October 13, 1906 US citizen Charles Magoon replaces Secretary of
War Taft as head of the provisional government of Cuba. The
United States openly rules "independent" Cuba for more than
two years.

January 28, 1909 US Military Governor Magoon turns the Cuban
government over to President José Miguel Gómez, an army
general elected in November 1908.

1912 The *Agrupación Independiente de Color* [Independent Colored
Party], led by Evaristo Estenoz who fought in the War of
Independence, rebels against the Gómez government, which
crushes the uprising with the slaughter of some 3,000 rebels.
During the uprising, US Marines land and two US battleships
anchor in Havana harbor but the Taft administration maintains

this does not constitute intervention.

February-March 1917   President Woodrow Wilson lands US Marines to shore up the government of President Mario García Menocal against an uprising led by Liberal Party forces because of what they consider the fraudulent victory of the Conservative Party in the 1916 election.

April 7, 1917   President Mario García Menocal enters World War I the day after the United States declares war and soon opens up the island as a training base for US Marines, some of whom remain until 1922.

1919-1933   During Prohibition in the United States, Cuba becomes the playground of the Caribbean. In 1920, sugar prices plunge and US investors buy up property at bargain rates.

March 13, 1925   After a delay of more than two decades, the US Senate ratifies the 1904 treaty relinquishing US claims to the Isle of Pines.

May 29, 1934   Cuba and the United States sign the "Treaty on Relations between Cuba and the United States" abrogating the "Permanent Treaty" of 1903 and the Platt Amendment with the exception that the United States continues to occupy the naval base at Guantánamo [see Document 7].

March 10, 1952   Batista comes to power as a result of a military coup.

January 1, 1959   Rebel forces led by Fidel Castro overthrow the Batista dictatorship.

March 5, 1959   Cuba demands that the US government give up its naval base at Guantánamo. This occupation of Cuban territory continues as a source of tension between the two countries. Cuba adopts a policy of not cashing the yearly checks for lease of the territory. The original annual rent of $2,000 in gold later becomes $4,085 (not in gold).

April 4, 1960   A plane flying out of the US naval base at Guantánamo drops incendiary material in Oriente province.

October 14, 1960 The US government presents a 10,000-word document to the United Nations in response to Prime Minister Castro's UN speech in September. The document blames Cuba for worsening relations. For example, the United States claims the right to occupy territory at Guantánamo because of the 1934 treaty, and states that there have been "only" five unauthorized flights over Cuba of which the US government possesses any "substantial" evidence.

January 12, 1961 Cuba reports the torture by US soldiers of Manuel Prieto, a worker at the Guantánamo Naval Base.

April 17, 1961 The United States finances and organizes a military invasion of Cuba at the Bay of Pigs which is rapidly defeated.

July 26, 1961 This is one of the dates earmarked for assassination of Fidel Castro, Raúl Castro and Che Guevara, according to a CIA plan, "Operation Patty," discovered by Cuban security forces. Seventeen years later at an International Tribunal in Havana, Humberto Rosales Torres, who had been arrested for his part in the plot and given a nine-year prison term, testifies that the plan also included a fake attack on the Guantánamo Naval Base that would have provided an excuse for sending in the US Marines.

October 15, 1961 Rubén López Sabariego, a Cuban worker at the US naval base at Guantánamo who was arrested on September 30, dies. Cuba says the cause is torture. In 1963, US columnist Jack Anderson reports that US Marine Captain Arthur J. Jackson was secretly dismissed because of the killing. The United States maintains that Jackson acted in self-defense and that his dismissal was kept secret to avoid international repercussions.

January 3, 1962 In a diplomatic note to the US government, Cuba protests 119 violations of its territory, 76 by planes from Guantánamo Naval Base.

March 20, 1962 By diplomatic note, Cuba protests to the US government about repeated provocations by soldiers at the US naval base in Guantánamo, Cuba.

April 9, 1962 Cuba sends another diplomatic note to protest provocations by US soldiers at Guantánamo Naval Base. These incidents are in addition to continual aerial and naval bombardment, sabotage of crops and industry, occasional landings along the coast, and assassinations.

June 1962 In daily radio broadcasts, Cuba maintains that the US government is using Guantánamo Naval Base for espionage and violation of Cuban territory.

July-October 1962 Aggression against Cuba is an everyday occurrence, including the killing of peasants in the Escambray; the killing of fisherman Rodolfo Rosell Salas by US soldiers from the Guantánamo Naval Base; the killing of a soldier and a militiaman by infiltrators; shots fired, sometimes for several hours, from Guantánamo Naval Base into the surrounding area; hit-and-run attacks by boats along the coast and other constant violations of Cuban territory by boats and planes that carry out espionage, sabotage, hijackings of boats, kidnappings, and infiltration of CIA operatives. Cubans capture many of the infiltrators.

October 2, 1962 In a memo to the Joint Chiefs of Staff, Defense Secretary Robert McNamara describes situations that might require US military force against Cuba, including placement of offensive weapons from the Soviet bloc in Cuba, a Cuban attack against Guantánamo Naval Base or US planes or vessels outside Cuban territory, assistance by Cuba to "subversion" in other countries of the Western Hemisphere, a request for assistance by leaders of a "substantial popular uprising" in Cuba or a "decision by the president that the affairs in Cuba have reached a point inconsistent with continuing US national security." The memo requests that contingency plans emphasize removal from power of Prime Minister Castro.

October 16-22, 1962 President Kennedy and his closest advisers deliberate on what to do about Cuban sites for nuclear weapons that could be used against the United States. On October 16, Attorney General Robert Kennedy discusses the idea of using the US naval base at Guantánamo in some way that would justify an invasion: "We should also think of, uh, whether there is some other way we can get involved in this through, uh, Guantánamo Bay, or something, or whether there's some ship that, you know, sink the *Maine* again or something."

October 28, 1962 After days at the nuclear brink, the worst of the Missile Crisis ends when Moscow Radio broadcasts Premier Khrushchev's letter to President Kennedy accepting the October 27 proposal. Concerning US aggression against Cuba, Khrushchev's letter says, "I regard with respect and trust the statement you made in your message of 27 October 1962 that there would be no attack, no invasion of Cuba, and not only on the part of the United States, but also on the part of other nations of the Western Hemisphere, as you said in your same message. Then the motives which induced us to render assistance of such a kind to Cuba disappear." Without consultation with Cuba, the Soviet Union begins dismantling the missile sites and withdrawing its missiles. At this point Prime Minister Castro asserts Cuba's position with a demand that the US government end five practices: the embargo, subversive activities inside Cuba, armed attacks against Cuba, violation of Cuban air and naval space, and occupation of Cuban territory at Guantánamo.

November 16, 1962 Responding in the UN General Assembly to a Brazilian initiative, supported by the US government, for the denuclearization of Latin America, Carlos Lechuga, who became Cuba's UN ambassador on October 31, says the nuclear powers should guarantee no use of nuclear weapons in Latin America and close their military bases there. He points out the illogic of allowing the US government to have a base at Guantánamo on Cuban territory while Cuba is not allowed to have a base belonging to a friendly country for its defense.

February 6, 1964 In reprisal for the US seizure of Cuban fishing boats, Cuba shuts off the normal water supply to the US naval base at Guantánamo, stating the suspension will continue until the United States releases the 38 Cubans.

February 7, 1964   President Johnson orders the Defense Department to discharge any of the 2,500 Cuban civilian employees at Guantánamo Naval Base who do not choose to live there or spend their earned dollars there. Water shuttles operate between Jamaica and the base. Four days later 700 Cuban workers are dismissed. A desalinization plant that can process more than a million gallons of water a day is built on the base.

June 12, 1964 Amid continuing attempts at undermining the Cuban government, Armed Forces Minister Raúl Castro reports that US troops at the Guantánamo Naval Base alone have been responsible for 1,651 acts of provocation since November 1962.

July 19, 1964 Cuban Frontier Guard Ramón López Peña is killed by US soldiers at the Guantánamo Naval Base.

October 5-11, 1964 The second summit of the Movement of Nonaligned Countries meets in Cairo and issues a final communiqué that includes a demand that the United States cease its occupation of Cuban territory at Guantánamo.

December 11, 1964 Che Guevara addresses the UN General Assembly in New York. Guevara demands an end to the US military occupation of Cuban territory at Guantánamo.

May 21, 1966 Luis Ramírez López, a Cuban frontier guard at Guantánamo, is shot dead, and Cuba's Armed Forces Ministry charges that the gunfire came from the US naval base at Guantánamo. The Cuban ministry says there was sporadic rifle fire from the base for about two hours. The US Defense

Department at first flatly denies the shooting but later says it is investigating.

November 19, 1968 Two US Marines based at Guantánamo Naval Base are captured on Cuban territory outside the base.

October 22, 1974 "CBS Reports" hosted by Dan Rather presents to a US television audience an interview with Prime Minister Castro. Regarding negotiations between Cuba and the United States, Castro says: "Guantánamo is a piece of Cuba's national territory. It is occupied by the United States. But we do not say that in order to start discussions they must withdraw from Guantánamo. Rather we have posed a single condition: that the economic embargo be ended."

May 30, 1977 Cuba and the United States agree to establish "interests sections" in each other's countries beginning September 1. These will deal primarily with trade and consular matters and will serve as channels of communication. As obstacles in the way of normalization of relations, the Carter administration cites Cuba's insistence that US troops stop occupying Cuban territory at the Guantánamo Naval Base.

December 24, 1977 Noting some improvement in relations with the United States during the Carter administration, President Castro responds to US criticism of Cuban troops in Angola, and asks, "What moral basis can the United States have to speak about our troops in Africa when their own troops are stationed right here on our own national territory at the Guantánamo Naval Base?"

October 1, 1979 In a television address, President Carter states his "reaffirmation" of President Kennedy's 1963 declaration "that we would not permit any troops from Cuba to move off the island of Cuba in an offensive action against any neighboring country." He lists five things his administration will do: increase surveillance; aid any country in the Western Hemisphere against "any threat from Soviet or Cuban forces";

establish a Caribbean Joint Task Force Headquarters at Key West; stage more military maneuvers and maintain US forces in Guantánamo; and increase economic aid to the Caribbean. On the same day, 16 US Navy ships arrive off Cuba for maneuvers and the Pentagon announces that it will stage an amphibious assault at Guantánamo.

Mid-April, 1980   International news agencies report that the Carter administration plans massive military maneuvers, "Operation Solid Shield 80," in the Caribbean starting May 8. Civilian personnel would be evacuated while US Marines land at Guantánamo as 1,200 US soldiers are transported there. Protesters in many countries, including the United States, demonstrate against such maneuvers.

May 1, 1980   At the May Day celebration, President Castro calls the cancellation of US maneuvers at Guantánamo a victory and suspends the "Girón 19" maneuvers that Cuba had planned for May 7.

May 19, 1980   Cuban officials say they are willing to discuss the US proposal for an airlift if negotiations include the embargo, the US occupation at Guantánamo, and spy flights.

July 31-August 3, 1980   Mexican President José López Portillo makes a state visit to Cuba and issues a joint communiqué with President Castro demanding that the US government end the embargo, violations of Cuban air space, and the military occupation at Guantánamo.

April 29, 1982   The US Defense Department begins military maneuvers in the Caribbean, one of eight such exercises since last October. "Operation Ocean Venture 82" will last until mid-May with participation from 45,000 troops, 350 planes and 60 ships, including a mock invasion of Puerto Rico and a "non-combatant evacuation operation" at Guantánamo Naval Base.

November 1, 1983   The US Defense Department says a nine-ship task force headed by the aircraft carrier *America* is not headed for the Caribbean but for the "Central Atlantic." But on November 3, the navy says the task force will arrive in the Caribbean within 24 hours for military maneuvers off Guantánamo Naval Base.

March 22, 1984 The US Defense Department announces that it will hold the largest military exercise of 1984 in the Caribbean April 20–May 6, including reinforcement of the Guantánamo Naval Base and a simulated evacuation of dependents. On the following day, Moscow announces that a squadron of Soviet warships will arrive in Cuba on March 25.

May 14, 1984 A Pentagon report, presented to Congress in early May and made public today, describes plans to spend $43.4 million to improve Guantánamo Naval Base during the next four years. The plans are part of an overall design for upgrading and constructing military installations in Central America and the Caribbean through 1988 while conducting constant military maneuvers in and around Honduras.

October 31, 1985 Asked during an interview by Soviet journalists if the United States would leave Guantánamo Naval Base if the Cuban people were to vote in a referendum that it should leave, President Reagan answers, "No, because the lease for that was made many years ago, and it still has many years to run, and we're perfectly legal in our right to be there. It is fenced off. There is no contact with the people or the main island of Cuba at all."

March 21, 1987 US officials announce plans for the largest military maneuvers yet in the Caribbean and Central America, including a simulated evacuation of Guantánamo Naval Base. The main goal of "Solid Shield '87" is to practice response to a Honduran call for assistance against an invasion by Nicaragua. The exercise at Guantánamo is to practice response to Cuba's projected reaction to the invasion of Nicaragua. After this announcement, the Soviet Union sends five submarines to hold an exercise in April in the western Atlantic near Bermuda, the largest deployment in that area since 1985. NATO officials say that four or five long-range Soviet bombers arrive in Cuba for this exercise.

January 18, 1988   US Secretary of the Navy James H. Webb, Jr., writes in a *Wall Street Journal* article that "it is reasonable to assume that we will lose our lease on Guantánamo Bay in 1999."

April 1-22, 1988   The US Defense Department stages military maneuvers, "Ocean Venture '88," in the Caribbean with 40,000 troops, 28 warships and dozens of aircraft. Evacuation of US residents is rehearsed at the Guantánamo Naval Base. "Ocean Venture" maneuvers take place every other year, alternating with "Solid Shield."

January 23, 1990   The US battleship *Wisconsin* arrives at Guantánamo Naval Base. Along with the earlier arrival of the amphibious assault ship *Wasp*, this constitutes a considerable buildup of US military force on Cuban territory.

April 29, 1990   Cuba's Defense Ministry announces that the US Defense Department will conjoin three threatening military maneuvers in early May. In previous years there have been large consecutive maneuvers in April, May and June, but this year "Ocean Venture," which began April 20, will coincide with "Global Shield" while Guantánamo Naval Base practices evacuation of civilian personnel.

September 11, 1991   Soviet President Gorbachev announces he intends to withdraw the Soviet training brigade from Cuba. The Cuban Foreign Ministry states that Gorbachev's remarks "were not preceded by consultations or any prior notice, which constitutes inappropriate behavior from the point of view of international standards as well as the agreements existing between the two states." Bush administration officials say they hope this will lead to the downfall of President Castro. On the following day, Soviet Foreign Minister Boris Pankjin says the Soviet Union wants the United States to match the Soviet military withdrawal from Cuba by removing US troops from Guantánamo Bay and halting military maneuvers in the region.

September 22, 1991 Responding to the Soviet plan to remove troops from Cuba, in a long editorial *Granma* reports the history of the Soviet brigade in Cuba and its relationship to the US military occupation of Cuban territory at Guantánamo. The editorial states that "we could be moving toward a world order in which small Third World countries like Cuba, whose social system is not to the liking of the United States, have no alternative except to risk disappearing; and in which there is no room for ideological loyalties or even the most elemental ethical principles, without which our civilization will be threatened with the possible emergence of a new barbarism based on US technological might and hegemonic delirium."

November 1991 The Pentagon builds housing for the flood of refugees arriving at the Guantánamo base from Haiti. In 1994, thousands of would-be Cuban emigrants join them. Eventually, more than 45,000 Cubans and Haitians are held in tent cities covering much of the base. Most Cubans are admitted into the United States, but most Haitians are sent back home. The last of the Cubans depart in 1996.

September 7, 1992 The final declaration of the 10th summit meeting of the Movement of Nonaligned Countries demands an end to the US military occupation of Guantánamo. Forty heads of state and 95 delegations are present.

August 30, 1994 In a *Wall Street Journal* opinion piece, Elliott Abrams suggests creating at Guantánamo Naval Base "a West Berlin, a small free city within the communist nation," the "embryo of a Guantánamo Bay Free Trade Zone." Then, in an interview with editors and reporters at the *Record*, a newspaper in his New Jersey district, Representative Torricelli urges Cuban Americans to turn the base into the site of a government in exile.

January 6, 1995 As US authorities begin the forced repatriation of Haitian refugees held at Guantánamo, Arthur Helton, professor of immigration law at New York University's Law School, tells the *New York Times* that although the US lease of the base remains in force, the land is part of Cuba under international law. He says, "The United States is trying to compel foreign nationals to return to their home country from a third country, which is an unprecedented assertion of sovereign power."

March 25, 1995 Cuba signs the 1967 Treaty of Tlatelolco. As a condition for Cuba's remaining within the treaty, it maintains that the US government should cease sending ships carrying nuclear weapons to Guantánamo Naval Base on Cuban territory. Cuba favors the destruction of all nuclear weapons as the only guarantee against their use and argues "the ones who should respect this principle first are the so-called nuclear powers."

May 2, 1995 At the press conference to announce the migration agreement between Cuba and the United States, the commander-in-chief of the US Atlantic Command, General John Sheehan, says, "We're going to move the fleet training center out of Guantánamo Bay, Cuba, because we can do the same thing in the continental limits of the United States at lower cost." But he says the base remains "essential for strategic reach reasons."

April 1999 President Clinton considers plans to house thousands of Kosovo refugees at the Guantánamo base, but abandons the idea.

January 11, 2002 First group of 20 prisoners captured in the so-called war against terrorism arrives at Guantánamo Bay's Camp X-Ray, where they are housed in open-air cages with concrete floors. The International Committee of the Red Cross makes its first visit six days later.

January 18, 2002 President George W. Bush decides detainees' standing as terrorists disqualifies them from prisoner-of-war protection under the Geneva conventions.

January 22, 2002 After a Navy photo is released showing detainees in goggles and masks, Defense Secretary Donald Rumsfeld defends the detention and treatment of "committed terrorists."

January 27, 2002 Vice-President Cheney calls the detainees "the worst of a very bad lot. They are very dangerous. They are devoted to killing millions of Americans."

February 12, 2002 US officials say they envision a long-term prison camp at the Guantánamo base.

February 27, 2002 Almost two-thirds of detainees go on a hunger strike to protest a rule against turbans in the first organized act of defiance. US officials decide to allow the turbans.

March 21, 2002 The Bush administration announces new military tribunal regulations.

April 25, 2002 Construction of the new 410-bed Camp Delta is completed.

April 28, 2002 Detainees are moved from Camp X-Ray to Camp Delta, a more permanent detention center.

March 11, 2003 The Federal Appeals Court rules that the detainees have no legal rights in the United States.

May 9, 2003 Guantánamo hits its peak population of 680. (All told, the camp has processed 773 detainees, but 680 is the largest number of detainees there at one time.)

October 9, 2003 The Red Cross issues a public statement noting "deterioration in the psychological health of a large number of detainees."

February 15, 2006 A UN Report recommends closure of the Guantánamo prison.

October 17, 2006 President Bush signs the military commissions into law.

November 17, 2006 US military announces a plan to build a new compound on the base to hold the military commission proceedings.

December 7, 2006 The first detainees are transferred to the newly-constructed Camp Six.

June 28, 2008 "We're not going anywhere anytime soon," declares Navy Commander Jeffrey M. Johnston in newspaper reports. He states that he "gets upset" when people equate the closing of the detention center with a shutdown of this 45-square-mile base. The United States maintained this base long before the first detainees arrived in January 2002, he says. Johnston, Guantánamo's public works officer who requisitions the $4,085 annual payments to Cuba to "lease" the base, describes the military as a perfect tenant. "We don't bother the landlord. We don't (complain) when things go wrong. We pay our rent on time," Johnston says. "It's like an Eisenhower-era town: You can leave your door unlocked, no one uses bike locks, and you even have the Communist enemy to stare down," Johnston says. In the past year, a Taco Bell and an Irish pub have opened. There is also a Subway.

The US military has considered "in a very, very preliminary way" basing Marines at Guantánamo for rapid deployment elsewhere, says Navy Captain Mark Leary, Guantánamo's commanding officer. Even if "democratic change" comes to Cuba, the navy would probably still want to stay here, he says. "I think there's a good reason we've been here for 110 years. I don't think we would abandon this place."

January 22, 2009 President Obama issues three executive orders — one ordering the closure of the prison at Guantánamo Bay

in one year, another banning the use of controversial CIA
interrogation techniques, and one ordering the review of
detention policy options.

May 15, 2009 President Obama announces he will revamp, rather
than reject, the system of military tribunals that President Bush
created to try terrorism suspects.

July 21, 2009 The White House grants its Guantánamo closing
commission an extra six months to study the situation.

Dec. 16, 2009 President Obama signs a presidential memorandum
ordering Attorney General Eric Holder and Defense Secretary
Robert Gates to acquire the state prison in Thompson,
Illinois, as the $350 million replacement for Guantánamo.
Administration officials are forced to acknowledge that closing
the facility in Cuba will not occur in 2009 but will spill over
into 2010, possibly even late 2010.

June 7, 2010 *The Washington Post* reports that the US military has
spent at least $500 million in recent years on renovations to
the Guantánamo base, including $296,000 for a go-kart track,
records show. Add in spending for top-secret items and the
total cost easily soars toward $2 billion, in the first public
accounting of spending at the base since the first detainees
arrived in January 2002. The costs do not include the $150
million a year that it takes to run the 45-square-mile base. Since
January 2002, the Pentagon built the go-kart track, which sits
unused, and spent $249,000 for a volleyball court that now is
abandoned and $3.5 million for 27 playgrounds that often are
vacant, the *Post* reported. A cafe renovation cost $683,000 and
another $773,000 was spent to renovate a building to house a
KFC/Taco Bell restaurant. Millions more were spent on first-
rate sports facilities, including football and baseball fields.
Captain Steven Blaisdell, the base commander, defends the
spending as necessary for a remote base that must provide a
range of services.

June 25, 2010 The *New York Times* announces that the Obama administration has sidelined efforts to close the Guantánamo prison, making it unlikely that President Obama will fulfill his promise to close it before his term ends in 2013.

THE EMPIRE AND THE INDEPENDENT ISLAND

Fidel Castro

The history of Cuba during the last 140 years is one of struggle to preserve national identity and independence, and the history of the evolution of the US empire, its constant craving to appropriate Cuba and of the horrendous methods that it uses today to maintain its domination of the world.

1. THE IMPOSITION OF THE PLATT AMENDMENT

Under the "ripe fruit doctrine," formulated in 1823 by Secretary of State and later President John Quincy Adams, it was assumed the United States would inevitably attain control over our country, by the law of political influence, once colonial subordination to Spain had ended.

Under the pretext of blowing up the *Maine* — a still unexplained event which the United States exploited to wage war against Spain (as it did with the prefabricated Gulf of Tonkin incident in order to attack North Vietnam) — President William McKinley signed the Joint Resolution of April 20, 1898, stating "the people on the island of Cuba are and by right ought to be free and independent... [and] the United States herewith declares that it has no desire or intention to exercise sovereignty, jurisdiction or control over said island, except for pacification thereof, and it affirms its determination, after this has been accomplished, to leave the government and control of the island to its people." The Joint Resolution entitled the president to use force to remove the Spanish government from Cuba.

Colonel Leonard Wood, chief commander of the Rough Riders, requested the support of Cuban insurrectionists who had weakened and defeated the Spanish colonial army after enormous sacrifices. Wood and Theodore Roosevelt, second in command of the expansionist volunteers, landed in our country on the beaches close to Santiago de Cuba, after the brave but poorly utilized Spanish squadron and their Marine infantry on board had been destroyed by the US battleships. The Rough Riders had landed without horses.

Following the defeat of Spain, representatives of the queen regent of Spain and the president of the United States signed the Treaty of Paris on December 10, 1898, and, without consulting of the Cuban people, agreed that Spain should relinquish all claim of sovereignty over and title to the island and would withdraw from it. Cuba would then be occupied by the United States on a temporary basis.

Already appointed US military governor Army Major General Leonard Wood issued Military Order 301 of July 25, 1900, which called for a general election to choose delegates to a constitutional assembly that would be held in the city of Havana at noon on the first Monday of November in 1900, with the purpose of drafting and adopting a constitution for the people of Cuba.

On September 15, 1900, elections took place and 31 delegates from the National, Republican and Democratic Union parties were elected. On November 5, 1900, the Constitutional Convention held its opening session at the Irijoa Theater of Havana which on that occasion was given the name of Martí Theater.

General Wood, representing the president of the United States, declared the assembly officially opened. Wood advanced the intention of the United States government: "After you have drawn up the relations which, in your opinion, ought to exist between Cuba and the United States, the government of the United States will undoubtedly adopt the measures conducive to a final and authorized treaty between the peoples of both nations, aimed at promoting the growth of their common interests."

The 1901 Constitution stated in Article 2: "The territory of the Republic is composed of the Island of Cuba, as well as the islands and neighboring keys, which together were under Spanish sovereignty until the ratification of the Treaty of Paris on December 10, 1898."

Once the constitution was drafted, the time had come to define political relations between Cuba and the United States. To that end, on February 12, 1901, a committee of five members was appointed and charged with studying and proposing a procedure that would lead to the stated goal.

On February 15, Governor Wood invited the members of the committee to go fishing and hosted a banquet in Batabanó, the main access route to the Isle of Pines, as it was known then, also occupied at that time by the US troops which had intervened in the Cuban War of Independence. It was there in Batabanó that he revealed to them a letter from Secretary of War Elihu Root, containing the basic aspects of the future Platt Amendment. According to instructions from Washington, relations between Cuba and the United States were to abide by several guidelines. The fifth of these was that, in order to make it easier for the United States to fulfill such tasks as were placed under its responsibility by the above mentioned provisions, and for its own defense, the United States could acquire title, and preserve it, for lands to be used for naval bases and maintain these in certain specific locations.

Upon learning of the conditions demanded by the US government, the Cuban Constitutional Assembly on February

27, 1901, passed a motion opposing the US executive, eliminating therein the establishment of naval bases.

The US government made an agreement with Orville H. Platt, Republican senator from Connecticut, to present an amendment to the proposed Army Appropriations Bill that would make the establishment of US naval bases on Cuban soil a *fait accompli*.

In the amendment, passed by the US Senate on February 27, 1901, and by the House of Representatives on March 1, and sanctioned by President McKinley the following day, as a rider attached to the "Bill granting credit to the Army for the fiscal year ending on June 30, 1902," the article mentioning the naval bases read as follows:

> "Art. VII. — That to enable the United States to maintain the independence of Cuba, and to protect the people thereof, as well as for its own defense, the government of Cuba will sell or lease to the United States lands necessary for coaling or naval stations at certain specified points to be agreed upon with the president of the United States."

Article VIII adds: "The government of Cuba will embody the foregoing provisions in a permanent treaty with the United States." The speedy passage of the amendment by the US Congress was due to the circumstance of it coming close to the conclusion of the legislative term and to the fact that President McKinley had a clear majority in both houses so that the amendment could be passed without any problem. It became US law when, on March 4, 1901, McKinley was sworn in for his second presidential term.

Some members of the Constitutional Convention maintained the view that they were not empowered to adopt the amendment requested by the United States since this implied limitations on the independence and sovereignty of the Republic of Cuba. Thus, the military governor Leonard Wood hastened to issue a new military order on March 12, 1901, where it was declared that the convention was empowered to adopt the measures whose constitutionality was in question.

Other convention members, such as Manuel Sanguily, held the opinion that the assembly should be dissolved rather than adopt measures that so drastically offended the dignity and sovereignty of the people of Cuba. But during the session of March 7, 1901, another committee was appointed in order to draft an answer to Governor Wood; the presentation of this was entrusted to Juan Gualberto Gómez who recommended, among other things, rejecting the clause concerning the leasing of coaling or naval stations.

Juan Gualberto Gómez maintained the most severe criticism of the Platt Amendment. On April 1, he tabled a debate in which he challenged the document on the grounds that it contravened the principles of the Treaty of Paris and of the Joint Resolution. But the convention suspended the debate on Juan Gualberto Gómez's point and decided to send another committee "to ascertain the motives and intentions of the government of the United States about any and all details referring to the establishment of a definitive order to relations, both political and economic, between Cuba and the United States, and to negotiate with the government itself, the bases for agreement on those extremes that would be proposed to the convention for a final solution."

Subsequently, a committee was elected that would travel to Washington, made up of Domingo Méndez Capote, Diego Tamayo, Pedro González Llorente, Rafael Portuondo Tamayo and Pedro Betancourt; they arrived in the United States on April 24, 1901. The next day, they met with Root and Wood who had earlier traveled back to his country for this purpose.

The US government hastened to publicly declare that the committee would be visiting Washington on their own initiative, with no invitation or official status.

Secretary of War Root met with the committee on April 25

and 26, 1901, and categorically informed them that "the right of the United States to impose the much debated clauses had been proclaimed for three-quarters of a century in the face of the United States and European world and they were not willing to give it up to the point of putting their own security in jeopardy."

The US officials reiterated that none of the Platt Amendment clauses undermined the sovereignty and independence of Cuba; on the contrary, they would be preserved, and it was clarified that intervention would only occur in the case of severe disturbances, and only with the objective of maintaining order and internal peace.

The committee presented its report in a secret session on May 7, 1901. Within the committee there were severe differences of opinion about the Platt Amendment. On May 28, a paper drafted by Villuendas, Tamayo and Quesada was tabled for debate; it accepted the amendment with some clarifications and recommended the signing of a treaty on reciprocal trade.

This paper was approved by a vote of 15 to 14, but the US government did not accept that solution. Governor Wood said the United States would only accept the amendment without qualifiers, and presented the convention with an ultimatum that, since the Platt Amendment was "a statute passed by the legislature of the United States, the president is obliged to carry it out as it is. He cannot change or alter it, add or take anything out. The executive action demanded by the statute is the withdrawal of the US Army from Cuba, and the statute authorizes this action when, and only when, a constitutional government has been established which contains, either in its body or in appendices, certain categorical provisions, specified in the statute... Then if these provisions are found in the constitution, the president will be authorized to withdraw the army; if he does not find [these provisions], then he will not be authorized to withdraw the army..."

The US secretary of war sent a letter to the Cuban Constitutional

Assembly where he stated the Platt Amendment should be passed in its entirety with no qualifications, because in that way it would appear as a rider to the Army Appropriations Bill; he indicated that, otherwise, his country's military forces would not be pulled out of Cuba.

On June 12, 1901, during another secret session of the Constitutional Assembly, the incorporation of the Platt Amendment as an appendix to the Constitution of the Republic passed on February 21 was put to the vote; 16 delegates voted in favor and 11 voted against. Bravo Correoso, Robau, Gener and Rius Rivera were absent from the session, thereby abstaining from voting in favor of such a monstrosity.

The worst thing about the amendment was the hypocrisy, the deceit, the Machiavellianism and the cynicism with which the plan to take over Cuba was concocted, to the extent of publicly proclaiming the same arguments made by John Quincy Adams in 1823, about the apple which would fall because of gravity. This apple finally did fall, but it was rotten, just as many Cuban intellectuals had foreseen for almost half a century, from José Martí in the 1880s right up to Julio Antonio Mella, who assassinated in January 1929.

There is no one better than Leonard Wood himself to describe what the Platt Amendment would mean for Cuba. In two parts of a confidential letter to his co-conspirator in the adventure, Theodore Roosevelt, dated on October 28, 1901, he writes:

> "There is, of course, little or no independence left Cuba under the Platt Amendment... the only consistent thing to do now is to seek annexation. This, however, will take some time, and during the period which Cuba maintains her own government, it is most desirable that she should be able to maintain such a one as will tend to her advancement and betterment. She cannot make certain treaties without our consent... and must

maintain certain sanitary conditions... from all of which it is quite apparent that she is absolutely in our hands, and I believe that no European government for a moment considers that she is otherwise than a practical dependency of the United States, and as such is certainly entitled to our consideration... With the control which we have over Cuba, a control which will soon undoubtedly become possession... we shall soon practically control the sugar trade of the world... the island will... gradually become Americanized and we shall have in time one of the richest and most desirable possessions in the world."

2. THE ESTABLISHMENT OF THE GUANTÁNAMO NAVAL BASE AS A FRAMEWORK FOR US–CUBA RELATIONS

By the end of 1901, the electoral process that resulted in the triumph of Tomás Estrada Palma, without opposition and with the support of 47 percent of the electorate, had begun. On April 17, 1902, the president-elect *in absentia* left the United States for Cuba where he arrived three days later. The inauguration of the new president took place at noon on May 20, 1902. The Congress of the Republic had already been constituted. Leonard Wood set sail for home in the battleship *Brooklyn*.

In 1902, shortly before the proclamation of the republic, the US government informed the newly elected president of the island about the four sites selected for the establishing of naval bases — Cienfuegos, Bahía Honda, Guantánamo and Nipe — as provided by the Platt Amendment. Not even the Port of Havana escaped consideration since it was contemplated as "the most favorable for the fourth naval base."

From the beginning, despite its spurious origins, the government of Cuba, which included many of those who had fought for independence, was opposed to the concession of four naval bases since two were considered to be more than enough.

The situation grew more tense when the Cuban government toughened its stand and demanded the final drafting of the Permanent Agreement on Relations, with the goal of "determining at the same time, and not in parts, all the details that were the object of the Platt Amendment and setting the range of their precepts."

President McKinley had died in September 14, 1901, as a result of gunshot wounds he had sustained on September 6. Theodore Roosevelt had advanced to such a degree in his political career that he was already vice-president of the United States and so he assumed the presidency after the shooting of his predecessor. Roosevelt at that time did not deem it to be convenient to specify the scope of the Platt Amendment, so as not to delay the military installation of the Guantánamo base. Of particular concern was the defense of the Panama Canal in the Central American isthmus, the construction of which France had begun and later abandoned and which the voracious government of the empire intended to complete at all costs. Nor was he interested in defining the legal status of the Isle of Pines. Therefore, he abruptly reduced the number of naval bases under discussion, removed the Port of Havana suggestion and finally agreed to the concession of only two bases: Guantánamo and Bahía Honda.

Subsequently, in compliance with Article VII of the constitutional appendix imposed on the Constitutional Convention, the agreement was signed by the presidents of Cuba and the United States on February 16 and 23, 1903, respectively:

> "Article I. The Republic of Cuba hereby leases to the United States, for the time required for the purposes of coaling and naval stations, the following described areas of land and water situated in the Island of Cuba:"1st. In Guantánamo"... (A complete description of the bay and neighboring territory is made.)

"2nd. In Bahía Honda..." (Another similar description is made.)

This Agreement establishes:

"Article III. —While on the one hand the United States recognizes the continuance of the ultimate sovereignty of the Republic of Cuba over the above described areas of land and water, on the other hand the Republic of Cuba consents that during the period of the occupation by the United States of said areas under the terms of this agreement the United States shall exercise complete jurisdiction and control over and within said areas with the right to acquire for the public purposes of the United States any land or other property therein by purchase or by exercise of eminent domain with full compensation to the owners thereof."

On May 28, 1903, surveying began to establish the boundaries of the Guantánamo Naval Station. In the agreement of July 2, 1903, dealing with the same subject, the "Regulations for the Lease of Naval and Coaling Stations" was passed:

"Article I. —The United States of America agrees and covenants to pay the Republic of Cuba the annual sum of two thousand dollars, in gold coin of the United States, as long as the former shall occupy and use said areas of land by virtue of said agreement.

"All private lands and other real property within said areas shall be acquired forthwith by the Republic of Cuba.

"The United States of America agrees to furnish to the Republic of Cuba the sums necessary for the purchase of said private lands and properties and such sums shall be accepted by the Republic of Cuba as advance payment on account of rental due by virtue of said agreement."

The agreement that governed this lease, signed in Havana by representatives of the presidents of Cuba and the United States respectively, was passed by the Cuban Senate on July 16, 1903, ratified by the president of Cuba a month later on August 16, and by the president of the United States on October 2; after exchanging ratifications in Washington on October 6, it was published in the *Gazette of Cuba* on October 12.

On December 14, 1903, it was reported that four days earlier (on December 10) the United States had taken possession of the areas of water and land for the purpose of establishing a naval station in Guantánamo.

For the US government and navy, the transfer of part of the territory of the largest island in the Antilles was a source of great rejoicing and they intended to celebrate the event. Vessels belonging to the Caribbean Squadron and some battleships from the North Atlantic Fleet converged on Guantánamo.

The Cuban government appointed the head of public works of Santiago de Cuba to deliver that part of the territory over which it technically exercised sovereignty on December 10, 1903, the date chosen by the United States. He would be the only Cuban present at the ceremony and then only for a brief time since, once his mission was accomplished, without any toasts or handshakes, he left for the neighboring town of Caimanera.

The head of public works boarded the battleship *Kearsage*, which was a US flagship, where he met Rear Admiral Barker. At noon a 21-gun-salute was given and along with the tune of the Cuban national anthem, the Cuban flag which had been flying on board that vessel was lowered, and the United States flag was hoisted immediately on land at the point called Playa del Este, with an equal number of salvos, thus concluding the ceremony.

According to the articles of the agreement, the United States had to dedicate the leased lands exclusively for public use and was not able to establish any type of business or industry. Furthermore, the US authorities in this territory and the Cuban authorities mutually agreed to surrender fugitives from justice charged with crimes or misdemeanors subject to the laws of each party, as long as it was required by the relevant authorities.

Materials imported into the areas belonging to the naval stations for their own use and consumption would be exempt from customs duties, and any other kind of fees, to the Republic of Cuba.

The lease of these naval stations included the right to use and occupy the waters adjacent to the areas of land and water, to improve and deepen the entrances to them and their anchorages and for anything else that would be necessary for the exclusive use to which they were dedicated.

Even though the United States acknowledged the continuation of Cuba's definitive sovereignty over those areas of water and land, it would exercise, with Cuba's consent, "complete jurisdiction and domain" over those areas while they occupied them according to the other already quoted stipulations.

In the so-called Permanent Treaty of May 22, 1903, signed by the governments of the Republic of Cuba and the United States, future relations between both nations were detailed. What Manuel Márquez Sterling would call "the intolerable yoke of the Platt Amendment" was thus put firmly in place.

The Permanent Treaty, signed by both countries, was approved by the US Senate on March 22, 1904, and by the Cuban Senate on June 8 of that year, and the ratifications were exchanged in Washington on July 1, 1904. Therefore, the Platt Amendment was an amendment to a US law, an appendix to the Cuban Constitution of 1901 and a permanent treaty between both countries.

The experience of the acquisition of the Guantánamo Naval Base was useful in the application of measures in the Panama Canal that were equal or worse. In the US Congress, it is customary to introduce amendments whenever a law is being debated that is considered urgent because of its content and importance. This frequently obliges legislators to put aside or sacrifice any conflicting aspects. Such amendments have more than once affected the sovereignty for which our people have tirelessly struggled.

In 1912, Cuban Secretary of State Manuel Sanguily negotiated a new treaty with the US State Department whereby the United States would relinquish its rights over Bahía Honda in exchange for expanding the boundaries of the Guantánamo station.

That same year, when the uprising of the Partido de los Independientes de Color (Independent Party of Color) was brutally repressed by the Liberal Party government of President José Miguel Gómez, US troops came out of the Guantánamo Naval Base and occupied several towns in the former Oriente Province, near the cities of Guantánamo and Santiago de Cuba, under the pretext of "protecting the lives and properties of US citizens."

In 1917, during the uprising known as "La Chambelona" carried out by elements of the Liberal Party in Oriente who were opposed to the electoral fraud that resulted in the re-election of President Mario García Menocal of the Conservative Party, Yankee regiments from the base headed for various points in that province of Cuba under the pretext of "protecting the base's water supply."

3. THE FORMAL REPEAL OF THE PLATT AMENDMENT

The advent of the Democratic Party administration of Franklin Delano Roosevelt in the United States in 1933 opened the way for a necessary adjustment in the dominance that the United States exercised over Cuba. The fall of Gerardo Machado's dictatorship under the pressure of a powerful popular movement, and the subsequent installation of a provisional government headed by the university professor of physiology, Ramón Grau San Martín, were a serious obstacle to the achievement of the reforms demanded by the people.

On November 24, 1933, US President Roosevelt issued an official statement encouraging the intrigues of Batista and Sumner Welles, the US ambassador in Havana, against Grau's government. These included the offer to sign a new commercial treaty and repeal the Platt Amendment. Roosevelt said "any Provisional Government in Cuba in which the Cuban people show their confidence would be welcome." The impatience of the US administration to get rid of Grau was growing; from mid-November 1933 the influence of a young anti-imperialist, Antonio Guiteras, was increasing in the government, which would take many of its more radical steps in the weeks to come. It was necessary to swiftly overthrow that government.

On December 13, 1933, Ambassador Sumner Welles returned to Washington and was replaced five days later by Jefferson Caffery.

On January 13-14, 1934, Batista convened and presided over a military meeting at Camp Columbia, where he proposed to oust Grau and appoint Colonel Carlos Mendieta y Montefur; this was agreed to by the so-called Columbia Military Junta. Grau San Martín presented his resignation at dawn on January 15, 1934, and left for exile in Mexico on March 20. Thus, on January 18, 1934, Mendieta was installed as president after the coup d'état. Although the Mendieta administration had been recognized by the United States on January 23, in reality the fate of the country was in the hands of Ambassador Caffery and Batista.

The overthrow of Grau San Martín's provisional government in January 1934, as a result of internal contradictions and a whole series of pressures, maneuvers and aggressions wielded against it by imperialism and its local allies, represented a first and indispensable step toward the imposition of a pro-imperialist oligarchy as opposed to a genuine solution of Cuba's national crisis. The government headed by Mendieta took on the task of adjusting the bonds of the country's neocolonial dependency.

But neither the oligarchy reinstated in power, nor Washington, were in position to ignore the feelings of the Cuban people toward neocolonialism and its methods. Nor was the United States unaware of the importance of the support needed from Latin American governments—Cuba among them—in the already anticipated confrontation with other emerging imperialist powers such as Germany and Japan.

The new process would include formulas to ensure the renewed functioning of the neocolonial system. The "Good Neighbor" policy was very mindful of Latin American opposition to Washington's open interventionism in the hemisphere. The aim of Roosevelt's policy was to portray a new image in its hemispheric relations through the "Good Neighbor" diplomatic formula.

As one of the adjustment measures, on May 29, 1934, a new US-Cuba Relations Treaty, modifying the agreement of May 22, 1903, was signed by President Roosevelt, who was perhaps a distant relative of the other Roosevelt who had landed in Cuba with the Rough Riders.

Two days earlier, at 10:30 a.m on May 27, when US Ambassador Jefferson Caffery was getting ready, as was his custom, to leave his residence in the Alturas de Almendares, he was the target of an assassination attempt; three shots were fired by several unidentified individuals from a car. At noon the following day, May 28, after having dropped off the diplomat at the embassy and driving along Quinta Avenida in Miramar, the car assigned to the first secretary of the US Embassy, H. Freeman Matthews, was attacked by several individuals armed with machine guns in a car. One of them approached the chauffeur and told him tell Matthews he was giving him one week to get out of Cuba; he then smashed the windshield of the car and sped away.

These events revealing a general climate of hostility against the United States could have precipitated the signing of the new Relations Treaty that proposed the supposed end of the unpopular Platt Amendment. This new Relations Treaty provided for the suppression of the right of the United States to intervene in Cuba. It stated:

> "The United States of America and the Republic of Cuba, being animated by the desire to fortify the relations of friendship between the two countries and to modify, with this purpose, the relations established between them by the Treaty of Relations signed in Havana, May 22, 1903... have agreed upon the following articles:

> "Article 3. Until the two contracting parties agree to the modifications or abrogation of the stipulations of the agreement in regard to the lease to the United States of America of lands in Cuba for coaling and naval stations signed by the president of the Republic of Cuba on February 16, 1903, and by the president of the United States of America on the 23 of the same month and year, the stipulations of that agreement with regard to the naval stations of Guantánamo shall continue in effect in the same form and conditions with respect to the naval station at Guantánamo. So long as the United States of America shall not abandon the said naval station of Guantánamo or the two Governments shall not agree to a modification of its present limits, the station shall continue to have territorial area that it now has, with the limits that it has on the date of the signature of the present Treaty."

The United States Senate ratified the new Relations Treaty on June 1, 1934, and Cuba did so on June 4. Five days later, on June 9, ratifications of the Relations Treaty of May 29 of the same year were exchanged, and with that the Platt Amendment was formally repealed. But the Guantánamo Naval Base remained.

The new treaty legalized the de facto situation of the Guantánamo naval station, thus rescinding the part of the agreements of February 16 and 23 and July 2 of 1903 between the two countries relating to the lands and waters in Bahía Honda, and the part that referred to the waters and lands of the Guantánamo station was amended, in the sense that they were expanded.

The United States maintained its naval station in Guantánamo as a strategic surveillance and control site in order to ensure its political and economic predominance in the Caribbean and Central America and to defend the Panama Canal.

4. THE GUANTÁNAMO NAVAL BASE BEFORE 1959

After the signing of the Treaty of Relations of 1934, the territory of the "naval station" underwent a gradual fortification and equipping process until, in the spring of 1941, the base became established as an operational naval station that included a naval station, an air naval station and a Marines corps base and warehouse facilities.

On June 6, 1934, the United States Senate had passed a bill that authorized the secretary of the navy to sign a long-term contract with a company that would undertake to supply adequate water to the Naval Base in Guantánamo; however, prior to this, US plans already existed for the construction of an aqueduct to bring in water from the Yateras River.

Expansion continued, and by 1943 other facilities were constructed by contracting the Frederick Snare Company, hiring 9,000 civilian workers, many of them Cubans.

Another year of tremendous expansion of the military and civilian facilities on the base was 1951. In 1952, the US secretary of the navy decided to change the name of the US Naval Operating Base to "US Naval Base"; by that time its structure already included a training center.

The period between the end of 1937 and 1940 was characterized, from a political point of view, by the adoption of measures that allowed for elections for the Constitutional Assembly to be called and for them to take place. The reason why Batista agreed to these democratizing measures was that it was in his interest to move toward the establishment of a situation that would allow him to remain at the center of political decision making, and thus ensure the continuity of his power within the new order. At the beginning of 1938, the agreement between Batista and Grau to install a Constitutional Assembly was made public. The Constitutional Convention, inaugurated on February 9, 1940, concluded its sessions on June 8, 1940.

The constitution was signed on July 1, 1940, and promulgated on July 5. The new law of laws established that "the territory of the Republic consists of the Island of Cuba, the Isle of Pines and other adjacent islands and keys, which were under the sovereignty of Spain until the ratification of the Treaty of Paris on December 10, 1898. The Republic of Cuba shall not conclude or ratify pacts or treaties that in any form limit or undermine national sovereignty or the integrity of the territory."

The oligarchy would strive to prevent the materialization of the more advanced principles in this constitution or at least to do their utmost to restrict their application.

5. THE GUANTÁNAMO NAVAL BASE SINCE THE REVOLUTION

Since the triumph of the revolution in January 1959, the revolutionary government has denounced the illegal occupation of that part of our territory occupied by the United States. But at the same time, the United States has transformed the occupied territory of the Guantánamo Naval Base into a permanent source of threats, provocation and violation of Cuba's sovereignty, with the aim of creating obstacles for the victorious revolutionary process. The base has always been part of the plans and operations conceived by Washington to overthrow the revolutionary government.

All kinds of aggressions have come from the naval base. These include:

- Dropping of inflammable materials over free Cuban territory from planes flying out of the base.
- Provocations by US soldiers, including insults, the throwing of stones and cans filled with inflammable material and the firing of pistols and automatic weapons.
- Violations of Cuban jurisdictional waters and Cuban territory by US military vessels and aircraft from the base.
- Plans for provocations against the base that would provoke a large-scale armed confrontation between Cuba and the United States.

On January 12, 1961, Manuel Prieto Gómez, a worker who had been employed at the base for more than three years, was savagely tortured by Yankee soldiers on the Guantánamo Naval Base for the "crime" of being a revolutionary.

On October 15 that same year, the Cuban worker Rubén López Sabariego was tortured and subsequently murdered.

On June 24, 1962, Rodolfo Rosell Salas, a fisherman from Caimanera, was murdered by soldiers at the base.

Similarly, the devious intent of fabricating a provocation and deploying US troops in a "justified" punitive invasion of Cuba has always been a volatile element at Guantánamo Base. One example of this was during the so-called "Operation Mongoose," on September 3, 1962, when US soldiers stationed in Guantánamo shot at Cuban sentries.

During the [1962] Missile Crisis, the base was reinforced in terms of military technology and troops; manpower grew to more than 16,000 Marines. Given the decision of Soviet Prime Minister Nikita Khrushchev to withdraw the nuclear missiles stationed in Cuba without either consulting or informing the revolutionary government, Cuba defined the unshakable position of the revolution in what came to be known as the "Five Points." The fifth point demanded withdrawal from the Guantánamo Naval

Base. We were on the brink of a thermonuclear war, where we would be the prime target as a consequence of the imperial policy of taking over Cuba.

On February 11, 1964, President Lyndon B. Johnson reduced the number of Cuban personnel working at the base by approximately 700 workers. They also confiscated the accumulated retirement funds of hundreds of Cuban workers who had been employed on the base and illegally suspended payments of pensions to retired Cuban workers.

On July 19, 1964, in a blatant provocation made by US border guards against the Cuban border patrol sentries, Ramón López Peña, a young 17-year-old soldier, was murdered at close range while he was on guard duty in the sentry-box.

On May 21, 1966, in similar circumstances, soldier Luis Ramírez López was murdered by shots fired from the base.

In less than three weeks of the month of May 1980, more than 80,000 men, 24 vessels and some 350 combat aircraft took part in Solid Shield-80 exercises; this included the landing of 2,000 Marines at the Naval Base and the reinforcement of the facility with an additional 1,200 troops.

In October 1991, during the Fourth Communist Party Congress held in Santiago de Cuba, planes and helicopters from the base violated Cuban air space over the city.

In 1994, the base served as a support station for the invasion of Haiti; US Air Force planes used base airports for this invasion. More than 45,000 Haitian emigrants were kept on the base until mid-1995.

Also in 1994, the well-known rafters migration crisis occurred as a result of the tightening of the US economic blockade of Cuba and the tough years of the "Special Period," the non-compliance with the Migration Accords of 1984 signed with the Reagan administration, the considerable reduction in the number of visas granted and the encouragement of illegal emigration, including the Cuban Adjustment Act signed by President Johnson more than three decades earlier.

As a result of the crisis created, a declaration made by President Clinton on August 19, 1994, transformed the base into a concentration camp for the Cuban rafters, who numbered nearly 30,000 people.

Finally, on September 9, 1994, a Joint Communiqué was signed by the Clinton administration and the Cuban government that committed the United States to preventing the entry into its territory of intercepted illegal emigrants and to issuing each year a minimum of 20,000 visas to Cubans for safe travel to the United States.

On May 2, 1995, as part of these Migration Accords, the governments of Cuba and the United States also agreed to a Joint Declaration establishing the procedure for returning to Cuba all those who continued trying to illegally migrate to the United States and were intercepted by the US Coast Guard.

The specific reference to the illegal emigrants intercepted by the Coast Guards laid the basis for a sinister business: the trafficking of human beings. The murderous [Cuban Adjustment] Act was maintained, thus turning Cuba into the only country in the world subjected to such harassment. While approximately 250,000 people have safely traveled to that country, an incalculable number of women, children and people of all ages have lost their lives as a result of the prosperous trafficking of emigrants.

Following an agreement by the two governments that resulted from the migration crisis of 1994, regular meetings between the military commands of each side were initiated. On many occasions our sappers have put their lives in danger to save people who were crossing the restricted military zone in that area, sometimes even accompanied by children.

This Act, signed by President Clinton on March 12, 1996, in Title II ("Assistance to a Free and Independent Cuba") Section

201 relates to the "policy toward a transition government and a democratically-elected government in Cuba," establishes in its Point 12 that the United States must "be prepared to enter into negotiations with a democratically elected government in Cuba either to return the United States Naval Base at Guantánamo to Cuba or to renegotiate the present agreement under mutually agreeable terms." This was something worse than what had been proposed by military governor Leonard Wood, who had landed on foot along with Theodore Roosevelt near Santiago de Cuba: the idea of having an annexationist of Cuban descent administrating our country.

The war in Kosovo in 1999 resulted in a large number of Kosovar refugees. The Clinton government, embroiled in that NATO war against Serbia, made the decision to use the base to accommodate a number of them, and on this occasion, for the first time, Cuba was informed of the decision made. Our answer was constructive. Even though we were opposed to the unjust and illegal conflict, we had no grounds on which to oppose the humanitarian aid needed by the Kosovar refugees. We even offered our country's cooperation, if it should be needed, in terms of medical care or any other service they might require. In the end, the Kosovar refugees were never sent to the Guantánamo Naval Base.

The manifesto called "The Oath of Baraguá" of February 19, 2000, stated: "In due course, since it no longer constitutes a prioritized objective at this moment, even though the right of our people is very just and cannot be waived, the illegally occupied territory of Guantánamo must be returned to Cuba." At that time, we were involved in the struggle for the return of the kidnapped boy [Elián González] and the economic consequences of the brutal blockade of Cuba.

On September 18, 2001, President Bush signed US Congress legislation authorizing the use of force as a response to the

September 11 attacks. Bush used this legislation as a basis to sign a military order on November 13 of that same year that would establish the legal basis for arrests and trials by military tribunals of individuals who did not have US citizenship as part of the "war on terrorism."

On January 8, 2002, the United States officially informed Cuba that they would be using the Guantánamo Naval Base as a detention center for prisoners captured in the war in Afghanistan.

Three days later, on January 11, 2002, the first 20 detainees arrived, and the figure reached 776 prisoners coming from 48 countries. Of course no details were mentioned. We assumed they were Afghan prisoners of war. The first planes landing were full of prisoners, and included many more guards than prisoners. On the same day, the Cuban government issued a public declaration indicating its willingness to cooperate with medical assistance as required, or any other useful, constructive and humane measures that might be needed. I was personally involved in details concerning the note presented by the [Cuban] Ministry of Foreign Affairs in response to the US note. We could never have imagined at that moment that the US government was preparing to create a horrendous torture center at that base.

The socialist constitution proclaimed on February 24, 1976, had set forth in Article 11, section c): "The Republic of Cuba repudiates and considers as null and illegal those treaties, pacts or concessions signed under conditions of inequality or which disregard or diminish her sovereignty and territorial integrity."

On June 10, 2002, in an unprecedented process of popular consultation, the people of Cuba ratified the socialist character of the 1976 Constitution in response to the meddling and offensive statements by the president of the United States. Similarly, it mandated the National Assembly of People's Power to amend the constitution so that it would expressly state, *inter alia*, the irrevocable principle which must govern the economic, diplomatic and political relations of our country with other states, by adding to the same Article 11, section c): "Economic, diplomatic and political relations with any other state may never be negotiated under aggression, threat or coercion by a foreign power."

After the Proclamation to the People of Cuba was announced on July 31, 2006, the US authorities declared that while they do not want to see another migration crisis, they are proactively preparing to face such a crisis by considering the use of the Guantánamo Naval Base as a concentration camp for illegal migrants intercepted on the high seas. In public statements, the United States has announced it is expanding the civilian buildings on the base with the aim of increasing the capacity to house illegal Cuban emigrants.

Cuba, for its part, has taken all possible measures to avoid incidents between the armed forces of both countries, and has declared that it is abiding by the commitments contained in the Joint Declaration on migration issues signed with the Clinton administration. So why has there been so much talk, threats and brouhaha?

The symbolic annual payment of $3,386.25 for the lease of the territory occupied by the Guantánamo Naval Base was maintained until 1972 when the North Americans adjusted it themselves to the sum of $3,676. In 1973, a new adjustment was made due to the change in the gold-US dollar exchange rate, and the check issued by the Treasury Department was increased to an annual payment of $4,085. That check is charged to the United States Navy, the party responsible for operations at the naval base.

The checks issued by the US government as payment for the lease are in the name of the "Treasurer General of the Republic of Cuba," an institution that ceased to function years ago within the structures of the Cuban government. This check is sent on a yearly basis, through diplomatic channels. The one for 1959, due to confusion, was included in the national budget. Since 1960, however, these checks have not been cashed and this is proof that the lease has been imposed against Cuba's will for more than 107 years. I would imagine, conservatively, that this annual payment is 10 times less than what the US government pays a schoolteacher each year.

Both the Platt Amendment and the Guantánamo Naval Base were unnecessary. History has shown that in a great many countries in this hemisphere, where there has not been a revolution and their entire territory is governed by the multinationals and the oligarchies, neither is necessary. Advertising has been the mechanism used to manipulate the minds of generally uneducated and poverty-stricken populations.

From the military point of view, a nuclear aircraft carrier, with so many fast fighter-bombers and escort ships supported by technology and satellites, is several times more powerful and can move to any point on the globe, wherever the empire requires it.

The US base at Guantánamo was necessary in order to humiliate and to carry out the dirty deeds that take place there. If we must await the downfall of the system, we will wait. The suffering and risks for humanity will be considerable, like the effects of today's stock market crisis, and this is predicted by a growing number of people. Cuba will always be waiting in a state of combat readiness.

GUANTÁNAMO:
A CRITICAL HISTORY

Roger Ricardo

Having no official land border with any other country, Cuba, the largest island in the Antilles, is separated by the Caribbean Sea and the Atlantic Ocean from its nearest neighbors: Mexico, the United States, the Bahamas, Haiti and Jamaica. Yet Cuba still has a small piece of territory encircled by barbed wire, extensive land mines, and occupied by hostile troops under a foreign flag. This occupied territory is the Guantánamo Naval Base, the oldest US overseas military installation. This strip of land in the southeastern corner of Cuba is a place of symbols and contrasts.

A sign proclaims "Republic of Cuba. Free territory in the Americas." Facing it, a few steps farther on, is the emblem of the US Marine Corps. The northeast gate provides the only access to the base from unoccupied Cuban territory, flanked by a sentry box where Marines keep watch. A few dozen meters away is the sentry box of the border patrol of the Cuban armed forces.

Every workday, a few elderly Cubans enter the base through that gate in the morning and leave through it at night; they are all who are left of the thousands of Cuban workers once employed on the base. Tension and acts of provocation by the US forces led most of the Cuban workers to leave; others were expelled.

This area wasn't richly endowed by nature, but the landscape is nevertheless quite striking: dozens of watchtowers and observation posts—both Cuban and US—stand as sentinels in the barren land, with kilometer upon kilometer of metal fences dividing "them" from "us." In between, there is a no-man's-land. Further inside the base, aircraft carriers, battleships, cruisers, destroyers, frigates, submarines, amphibious craft, helicopter carriers and Coast Guard vessels go busily in and out of the immense bay. The bay has 42 anchorages—enough for an entire war fleet.

At the back of the bay, on the Cuban side, are two towns: Caimanera and Boquerón. Theirs was a sad history until 1959, as US troops from the base used them as enormous brothels—a shameful and offensive situation for the Cuban population which the revolution promptly ended. Now the ports of these towns are used for shipping sugar and for fishing. Cargo ships must reach them via an international channel that passes the gunboats and proving grounds for the planes and artillery of the US Marine Corps. However, the channel is often closed to peaceful shipping—whenever it suits the interests of those who believe themselves the lords and masters of the bay.

The US State Department emphasizes that the main reason for the Guantánamo base is political. In its view, the greatest power on earth shouldn't have to cede to pressure from a small, poor, communist country. The US Navy adds that Guantánamo is the largest and best base in the world for training purposes.

The weather is nearly always fine and warm in Guantánamo, with an average annual rainfall of 12 inches. The port can accommodate the largest ships in the US Navy; 10 minutes sailing from the mouth of the bay, the water is 100 fathoms deep. There is little sea and air traffic in the area, so maneuvers and artillery exercises can be conducted without concern. The recent increase in these practices on the base has led US families living there to protest against the incessant artillery fire, low-flying planes, constant alarms and troop movements.

It is estimated that over 13,000 acts of provocation by US troops have been carried out since 1962, demonstrating the anti-Cuban policy of successive US administrations.

TOOL FOR POLITICAL BLACKMAIL

Secret US government documents that were declassified in early 1992—foreign policy materials, intelligence assessments and diplomatic information from the 1,191-page *Foreign Relations of the United States, 1958–1960*, Volume VI, "Cuba"—reveal that the United States has been drawing up plans against Cuba for more than three decades, beginning just a month after the January 1959 triumph of the Cuban revolution. This document also contains the program of secret actions against Fidel Castro that the CIA prepared in late 1960. The way the United States is handling the sensitive question of the Guantánamo Naval Base is instructive.

Researchers and specialists from the United States and other countries suggest the base has lost its usefulness and is, in fact, quite vulnerable. Therefore, the return of the territory wouldn't affect the military plans of the US in any important way. The loss of the enclave's strategic value is evident, for most of the activities and installations have been duplicated at other US bases. Because of its location, the Guantánamo installation would theoretically play some role in case of a military blockade of Cuba, but its vulnerability suggests that it would not be essential.

Even though the base has such geographical advantages as deep water and rapid access to the exercise areas, it does not possess the strategic possibilities of other installations in the region. The proximity of Haiti, Jamaica and the Cayman Islands means that maneuvering possibilities in the Guantánamo area are more limited than at the proving grounds in northern Puerto Rico, Antigua and Barbados, which face the open Atlantic.

The southeastern approaches to the United States are protected by other US installations in the area and McDill and Homestead

Air Force Bases in Florida maintain air and naval patrols. Battle groups headed by aircraft carriers or destroyers protect the area's ports, demonstrating the navy's ability to redistribute its forces among its bases on the mainland and offer more dynamic and modern naval coverage for the main points of its coast.

It is clear that the Guantánamo base is, above all, a symbol of US power, with the United States controlling a portion of Cuba's territory against the will of its people. At the same time, the possibility of the base serving as a tool for blackmail—to obtain future concessions from Cuba—should not be ruled out. During the October 1962 Missile Crisis sources close to the White House stated that Adlai Stevenson, then US ambassador to the United Nations, had suggested to President Kennedy that he include Guantánamo in a possible proposal for reaching an agreement with the Soviet Union. But apparently the president had replied that the timing wasn't right. This indicates two things: the insignificant military value Guantánamo had at that time and its increasing role as a political tool.

It is important to note that Fidel Castro stated during that crisis that the withdrawal of US troops from the Guantánamo base and the return of the territory to its legitimate owners would provide Cuba with a guarantee that the United States would not wipe out the island. For Cuba, the presence of US troops in that enclave constitutes a threat to both international peace and security and its national security.

In diverse international forums, Cuba has called for respect for its rights and has been supported by the international community. For example, the Movement of Nonaligned Countries stated in its first summit conference, held in Belgrade in 1961, that "the US military base at Guantánamo, Cuba, the presence of which has been opposed by the government and people of Cuba, affects the sovereignty and territorial integrity of that country." In later meetings, that Third World organization ratified its support for

Cuba's demand. Within that context, some US political experts consider that the Guantánamo base should be returned because, since Cuba is a nonaligned country, it is obliged not to turn any of its territory over to another foreign country for use as a military base.

It should be noted that Cuba's call for the return of the area that the United States illegally occupies is based on the principle of sovereignty and implies opposition to any other similar situation. Cuba never had any intention of establishing a base there or of turning Guantánamo over to another foreign power if the United States had returned it—not even when the Soviet Union was cooperating militarily with Cuba. Cuba's agreements with the Soviet Union were always in accord with Cuba's foreign policy, which was based on the principles of independence and the defense of Cuban sovereignty.

With binoculars, you can see Cuba's unwelcome neighbor from El Picote hill, in the eastern sector of the Cuban border. The Guantánamo base covers an area of nearly 118 square kilometers, 49.4 of which are solid ground; 38.8, water; and 29.4, swampland. In the 1990s, around 7,000 people were stationed within the compound permanently; more than 3,000 were military personnel, and the rest, their families and support personnel. In addition, there is a floating population of thousands, such as crews in transit, the exact figure depending on the number and kind of ships in port.

The residents live in the Villamar, Bargo, Deer Point, Villamar Extension and other neighborhoods, depending on their social class and position in the military hierarchy. Sherman Avenue leads from the residential area to the port installations and other key areas of the base. Every month, several dozen ships of the US Fleet Forces Command [previously the Atlantic Fleet Command] and planes of various kinds enter and leave the base on supply, instruction and anti-drug trafficking missions, according to US authorities, although they also use this cover to keep a group that is ready to participate in any kind of military action in the Caribbean area. The US troops also engage in reconnaissance missions against Cuba.

The United States has two airfields in the base: McCalla [now inactive], to the east, and Tres Piedras, also called Leeward Point—the larger of the two—to the west. The proving ground for planes and target area for the artillery—155-mm howitzers emplaced at Cable Beach, to the east, and on Toro Norte and Toro Sur Cays—is also to the west, in the swampy San Nicolás area near the bay. Important military sites, such as command and observation posts and radar positions, are on the eastern heights.

The base has a hospital, warehouses, powder magazines, obstacle courses and shooting ranges for infantry and tanks, as well as quarters for the troops (such as Bulkeley). It also has a desalination plant that can process more than a million gallons of water a day. However, occasionally water has had to be brought from the United States. The desalination plant was built very quickly when the Cuban government cut off supplies of drinking water to the base on February 6, 1964, after US authorities had kidnapped and imprisoned 38 Cuban fishermen, and armed pirate vessels based in Florida had repeatedly attacked Cuban fishing boats.

Estimates in several US publications state that over $100 million has been spent on the base's installations. Even so, a budget of around $35 million was approved in 1992 to modernize and enlarge them—a sure sign of the US authorities' determination not to abandon this Cuban territory.

Thus, the US government is spending millions on Guantánamo—for which, under the lease signed in February 1903, it is supposed to pay $2,000 in gold coins a year for as long as it occupies the base (an amount worth around $4,085 a year in the mid-1990s). This means that for this huge area, the United States owes Cuba annual rent of less than a cent per square meter of land.

However, since the triumph of the revolution, the Cuban authorities have not cashed a single check from the US government for rent for the base, convinced that no money on earth could purchase Cuba's sovereignty over that illegally occupied territory. Those checks and the $14,000 a month that the United States used to pay for water supplied to the base were the only two financial links the United States maintained with Cuba when, in 1962, it imposed the harshest and longest economic blockade that one country has ever imposed against another in times of "peace."

These are the symbols and contrasts on the border, where only a few centimeters from the area occupied by the United States stands a royal palm, Cuba's national tree, straight and tall on the semi-desert plain asserting that this land is Cuban.

AN OLD DREAM, A LONG NIGHTMARE

A few weeks after his inauguration as president, Thomas Jefferson called his closest friends together to swap ideas about the future of the young, impetuous United States. In that meeting, Jefferson clearly defined one key aspect of his foreign policy when he said he had always viewed Cuba as the most interesting addition that could be made to the nation. The United States had for a long time cast covetous eyes on Cuba. Its expansionist intentions were manifest very soon after it obtained its own independence from England, when the Caribbean island was still a Spanish colony.

John Adams, second president of the United States, was the first US government leader to express what was to be the US attitude toward Cuba in the late 18th and all of the 19th century: Cuba should remain in Spanish hands until the time came when it could be seized by the United States. Above all, it should never be independent. In a letter to Robert R. Livingston, Adams wrote on June 23, 1783, that the Caribbean island was a natural extension of the American continent, and therefore it was impossible to resist the conviction that the annexation of Cuba to the federal republic was indispensable for the continuation of the Union.

In 1823, the US government outlined the two concepts that were to determine the relations between that nation and the neighboring Caribbean island: the doctrine of Manifest Destiny and the theory of the "ripe fruit." Both are based on the use of military might as a tool of foreign policy and the US determination to impose its way of life as the highest form of civilization—precepts which are apparently still pillars of US foreign relations.

John Quincy Adams, secretary of state in the Monroe administration and Monroe's successor as president, gave those concepts their most original formulation, employing the law of gravity from physics in his "ripe fruit" theory in the sphere of politics:

> ...if an apple, severed by the tempest from its native tree, cannot but fall to the ground, Cuba, forcibly disjoined from its unnatural connection with Spain and incapable of self-support, can gravitate only to the North American Union, which, by the same law of nature, cannot cast her off from its bosom.

Seven and a half decades after John Quincy Adams' prediction, the United States declared war on a battered and exhausted Spain— just when the Cuban patriots' independence army was about to achieve victory after 30 years of intermittent armed struggle against the Spanish crown. On April 11, 1898, President McKinley sent the US Congress his long-awaited message on US relations with Spain and the war in Cuba, requesting authorization to intervene in the conflict. The House of Representatives and Senate debated the issue for several days; on April 19, they issued their joint resolution. The next day, McKinley signed it into law, turning it into an ultimatum that triggered war with Spain.

The United States never recognized the Cuban people's struggle for independence, their governments-in-arms or their status as a legitimate party to the conflict. A few hours after declaring war on Spain, the US president said it would not be wise for the United States to recognize the independence of the so-called Republic of Cuba at that time because, if it were to do so and intervene, its conduct would be subject to the approval or disapproval of such a government; then it would have to either submit to its leadership or enter into a friendly alliance with it.

All this shows that the US interest in "liberating" Cuba was simply an expression of its determination to keep the island from becoming independent, and to sweep Spain out of the Caribbean and seize that area of influence for itself. The blowing up of the *Maine* in Havana Bay was engineered as a pretext for the United States to intervene in the war. The battleship, which had arrived in Cuba on a "courtesy visit," was blown up on February 15, 1898, and the war ended with the US military occupation of the island.

The US press at the time mounted an enormous campaign supporting the government's action. One newspaper, for example, carried a photograph showing what it claimed was the hole made in the *Maine* by a Spanish torpedo. Later, it turned out that the photo had been published the previous year—and was of an eclipse of the sun. Over 80 years had to pass before the US authorities acknowledged that the Spanish had not blown up the *Maine*. Then, US specialists admitted that the explosion had taken place on board, in a tiny ammunition store in the prow, as stated in Admiral Hyman G. Rickover's book *How the Battleship Maine was Destroyed*.

The US government's political pragmatism toward Cuba was expressed in its complete lack of respect for the Cuban people, as evident in a memo by Undersecretary of War J.C. Breckenridge [included as appendix 1 in this book]. Writing from Washington on December 24, 1897, to Lieutenant General Nelson A. Miles

of the US Army, who had been named general-in-chief of the
intervention forces, Breckenridge instructed him how to carry
out the war. He said that Cuba was larger and had a greater
population than Puerto Rico and that its population consisted
of whites, blacks, Asians and mestizos—who, in Breckenridge's
opinion, were generally indolent and apathetic. He said that,
naturally, the immediate annexation of those elements to the
US federation would be madness, and, before suggesting any
such thing, the US forces should cleanse Cuba—if necessary, by
employing the same means which Divine Providence applied to
Sodom and Gomorrah.

Specifically, Breckenridge argued that the United States
would have to destroy everything within range of its cannon and
mercilessly tighten the blockade so that hunger and pestilence, its
constant companion, would decimate Cuba's peaceful population
and reduce its army. The allied Cuban army should be employed
constantly in scouting forays; be always in the vanguard so that,
caught between two fires, it would bear the brunt of the war;
and be assigned all of the dangerous and hopeless expeditions.
Summing up, the note said that US policy should consist of always
supporting the weaker against the stronger until the extermination
of both Cubans and Spaniards had been attained and the United
States could annex the Pearl of the Antilles. He could hardly have
been more explicit.

In their efforts to prevent Cuba's independence, the US
authorities also had the support of certain economic circles on
the island, such as the sugar magnates, who had commercial
ties with their powerful neighbor. Both the owners of the Cuban
sugar industry—the country's main source of income—and the
government officials in Washington knew that the Cuban people
bitterly opposed annexation and were ready to continue fighting
rather than see another form of domination imposed. That factor
was largely responsible for the US authorities changing their

annexationist plan and their apparent acceptance of the Cuban people's desire for independence.

THE CUBAN RESPONSE

General Máximo Gómez, one of the fathers of Cuban independence who became commander-in-chief of the *mambí* liberation army, clearly expressed the Cuban people's thinking on the US military intervention. On January 8, 1899, he wrote in his campaign diary:

> The Americans' military occupation of the country is too high a price to pay for their spontaneous intervention in the war we waged against Spain for freedom and independence. The American government's attitude toward the heroic Cuban people at this history-making time is, in my opinion, one of big business. This situation is dangerous for the country, mortifying the public spirit and hindering organization in all of the branches that, from the outset, should provide solid foundations for the future republic, when everything was entirely the work of all the inhabitants of the island, without distinction of nationality.
>
> Nothing is more rational and fair than that the owner of the house should be the one to live in it with his family and be the one who furnishes and decorates it as he likes and that he not be forced against his will and inclination to follow norms imposed by his neighbor.
>
> All these considerations lead me to think that Cuba cannot have true moral peace — which is what the people need for their happiness and good fortune — under the transitional government. This transitional government was imposed by force by a foreign power, and therefore is illegitimate and incompatible with the principles that the entire country has been upholding for so long, and in the defense of which half of its sons have given their lives and all of its wealth has been consumed.

There is so much natural anger and grief throughout the island that the people have not really been able to celebrate the triumph of the end of their former rulers' power.

They have left in sadness, and in sadness we have remained, because a foreign power has replaced them. I dreamed of peace with Spain; I hoped to bid farewell with respect to the brave Spanish soldiers with whom we always met, face to face, on the field of battle. The words *peace* and *freedom* should inspire only love and fraternity on the morning of concord between those who were combatants the night before; but, with their guardianship imposed by force, the Americans have turned the Cubans' victorious joy to bitterness and have not sweetened the grief of the vanquished.

The situation that has been created for this people—one of material poverty and of grief because their sovereignty has been curbed—is ever more distressing. It is possible that, by the time this strange situation finally ends, the Americans will have snuffed out even the last spark of goodwill.

Within the space of eight months, Cuba saw US military intervention; the defeat of the Spanish crown; an end to the fighting; and a series of hostile actions taken by the interventionist forces against the Cuban independence fighters, who had really won the war.

The naval battle of Santiago de Cuba and the seizure of that city in southeastern Cuba were decisive acts in the course of the war and accelerated the peace negotiations. The Treaty of Paris [included as Document 2 in this book], which ended the war, was signed on December 10, 1898. The US authorities, who acted as if Cuba were a conquered country, negotiated with the Spanish colonial rulers, and both excluded the Cuban people's representatives from the peace talks. Tied hand and foot, Cuba was turned over to the United States.

President McKinley set forth the real US intentions concerning

Cuba in his December 5, 1899, message to Congress, in which he said Cuba had, of necessity, to be attached to the United States by special organic or conventional ties—fancy words for annexation and a formula that would guarantee it.

It did not take long for the president's wishes to be carried out. On March 2, 1901, while considering a military appropriations bill, the US Congress added an amendment [included as Document 3] authorizing the US president to leave the government and rule of the island of Cuba in the hands of the Cuban people. But this would only happen after a government had been established on the island under a constitution in which, either as an integral part or as an attached statute, the future relations of the United States with Cuba were to be outlined.

This became known as the Platt Amendment because it was presented by Senator Orville Platt, although it had been drafted by Secretary of War Elihu Root. Thus, the first bite was taken of what John Quincy Adams had called the "ripe fruit."

Under this amendment attached to the constitution, the United States limited Cuban sovereignty and turned Cuba into a neo-colony; it retroactively legalized US military intervention in the island; it assumed the right to seize a part of Cuba's national territory by leaving the ownership of the Isle of Pines (the second largest island in the Cuban archipelago, south of the Cuban mainland) to be adjusted by future treaty; it limited Cuba's right to enter into treaties, contract debts and even set up sanitation programs; and, most opprobrious of all, forced the country to sell or lease a part of its territory for the establishment of naval stations.

With the July 1903 Permanent Treaty [the Complementary Agreement on Coaling and Naval Stations, included as Document 5], a piece of Cuban territory was handed over to the United States— for which Cuba was to receive $2,000 in gold coins a year for as long as the United States should wish to occupy and use that area. Thus, the US Guantánamo Naval Base was born.

GUANTÁNAMO BAY

When Christopher Columbus sailed into Guantánamo Bay on April 30, 1494, during his second voyage to the New World, he named it Great Port, describing it in his diary as "a broad bay with dark water, of unsuspected dimensions." In 1500, however, when his cartographer made a map of the lands that had been discovered, he called it Guantánamo, because that is what the indigenous Cubans living near the bay called their region. They actually had a different name for the bay itself — Joa, after a cactus with a red fruit similar to a tomato that abounded in its vicinity.

No use was made of the magnificent port until 1741, when a squadron of the English fleet arrived and, under the command of the Admiral Edward Vernon, tried (in vain) to conquer the eastern part of Cuba from there. The men of the fleet left some fortifications on what, ever since, has been known as Loma de los Ingleses (Englishmen's Hill), and the beginning of a settlement which they called Cumberland — where, many years later, the present town of Caimanera was built.

The first contact the United States had with the bay was in June 1898, when Admiral Sampson seized it and landed around 600 Marines during the Spanish-Cuban-American War. On that occasion, the Spanish troops stationed in the area attacked the Marines soon after their landing and would have defeated them if it had not been for the Cuban liberation army, which entered the battle and kept the US forces from being crushed.

Paradoxically, the US forces' use of Guantánamo Bay was decided nearby, in Santiago de Cuba, after the fighting that led to the culmination of what Secretary of State John Hay, in a letter to President Roosevelt, was to call "the splendid little war."

On March 24, 1902, Tomás Estrada Palma, president of Cuba, and Theodore Roosevelt, president of the United States, met in the White House. Roosevelt told Estrada Palma which places had been chosen for establishing naval or coaling stations, as stipulated in clause VII of the Platt Amendment: Cienfuegos and Guantánamo, on the southern coast, and Nipe and Honda Bays, on the northern coast. Later, in the Permanent Treaty of 1903, reference was made only to the leasing of Guantánamo and Honda Bays.

On December 12, 1903, control of the Cuban territory on Guantánamo Bay that was to be leased was officially handed over to the United States in a ceremony held on board the battleship *Kearsage*, flagship of the squadron of the Atlantic Fleet. In accord with the note the Cuban government had sent to the United States, requesting that the ceremony be kept low key because the Cuban people were protesting against the lease, only one Cuban was present. At noon on that day, the Cuban flag was lowered while a 21-gun salute was fired, and the US flag was raised in its stead. That was all. Soon after, around 600 US troops landed.

Thus, the United States took possession of a key point in the Caribbean Sea, ensuring its military control of the area, control over the Panama Canal and the rapid deployment of its forces to any point in Central or South America. Theodore Roosevelt recognized the importance of Guantánamo when, in a message to Congress, he described it as the "absolutely necessary strategic base" for controlling the Caribbean and the route to the Panama Canal.

Not content with what it had obtained, in 1912 the United States imposed another agreement for extending the boundaries of Guantánamo in exchange for giving up Honda Bay — which, obviously, had little importance to its strategic plans. With that expansion, the United States could control nearly the entire bay — especially its access channel, although it had been agreed at first that the channel would be shared so as to guarantee free trade by the Cuban ports of Caimanera and Boquerón. This, too, was conceded under threat of intervention.

The US authorities used the Guantánamo base for their subsequent invasions of the Dominican Republic, Haiti, Nicaragua, Mexico and Panama — demonstrating the "Big Stick" policy in the first two decades of the 20th century.

In response to the Cuban people's unwavering opposition to the actions of the US authorities, the Cuban revolutionary process of 1933, and the economic crisis that scourged the United States at the time, President Franklin D. Roosevelt proposed the "Good Neighbor" policy. The application of this concept in US foreign policy toward the rest of the hemisphere had repercussions in Cuba with the 1934 signing of the Treaty of Relations [see Document 7]. While that document repealed the Platt Amendment and the Permanent Treaty of 1903, it maintained all the stipulations concerning the leasing of the Guantánamo base — that is, it left the running sore of Cuban-US relations to fester.

Moreover, at the same time the document establishing the US "Good Neighbor" policy toward Cuba was being signed in Washington, over 20 US warships of the Atlantic Fleet made a "friendly visit" to the Bay of Havana and other points along the island's coasts.

Some say that words on paper are one thing, and their application another. The same could well be said of the history of US policy toward Cuba, in which the Guantánamo base is an excellent example. A joint resolution of the House and Senate of the United States declared that the Cuban people were and by right ought to be free and independent and that the United States had no intention or desire of exercising sovereignty, jurisdiction or rule in Cuba except for the purpose of pacifying the island.

In the Treaty of Paris, the US government stated that, as long as its occupation of the island of Cuba should last, it would assume and fulfill the obligations under international law to protect life and property. The Paris meeting was followed by the July 25, 1900, constitutional convention in Cuba, which was to implement the joint resolution by drafting the constitution and agreeing to the stipulations concerning bilateral relations between the United States and Cuba.

The Platt Amendment was attached to a military appropriations bill in the United States on March 2, 1901 — many months after the Cuban constitutional convention had been called, its members had been empowered to draft the Cuban constitution and they had concluded their deliberations.

At that time, Enrique Villuendas, one of the members of the constitutional convention, stated: "The amendment demands of the members of the convention that we accept conditions, but when the Cuban people voted to confer on us the mandate contained in the call for the convention, they asked only for wording and style." Thus, as an appendix to the constitution, the Platt Amendment is unconstitutional — and, therefore, everything emanating from it cannot be legally binding.

Coercion and fraud were constants in the process leading to the establishment of the US military enclave in Cuba — factors that, under international law, make any agreement null and void. The following example is very eloquent. In a letter to Secretary Root, General Leonard Wood, US military governor of Cuba, wrote that the time had come to establish the position of the government with absolute clarity and that it should be done in the form of an ultimatum, so that all discussion would cease.

General Wood also warned the Cuban convention that it should not modify the amendment and that the US troops would not leave Cuba until the terms of the amendment had been adopted. So there should be no possible misunderstanding, his warning wound up by saying that, if the amendment were not accepted, there would be no republic. Clearly, consent was obtained under duress.

SOVEREIGNTY AND THE LAW

International law establishes the principle of consent as the basis for any legal obligation resulting from an agreement. The agreements on the Guantánamo base should be annulled by reason of lack of consent, since that precept was not observed. Likewise, consent is determined by the aim and cause. The question arises of what became of the cause of maintaining Cuba's independence — which was put forward at the beginning of the century — and of what, in the light of facts past and present, happened with the friendship between the two countries.

A further example of the violation of international legal norms are the terms of the lease of the bay. The agreements ignore the temporary nature of any lease and express an intention to lease it in perpetuity. In fact, it is absurd to think that the owner of anything that is leased cannot recover it at a given time, because any lease is, *per se*, temporary.

Moreover, international law consecrates the precept of basic changes of circumstance, which means that, when the circumstances which gave rise to an agreement change, the agreement may be considered ineffective, inapplicable or null and void. It is obvious that, after the triumph of the revolution in 1959, the base became a tool of aggression, not friendship.

Therefore, the base should have been returned to Cuba in January 1961, when the United States broke off diplomatic relations with the island. At the time, however, the Eisenhower administration stated unilaterally that the United States would retain the base, abrogating to itself the right of decision that pertained to the government with which it was breaking its ties.

At the beginning of the century, the Guantánamo Naval Base was of strategic importance to US military policy, and that importance was the reason for its creation. Now, this is no longer the case. Nor does the pretext of the East-West confrontation any longer exist. Therefore, the Cuban government regards the

US retention of the base as an unmitigated act of force and a permanent offense to Cuba's national dignity and sovereignty.

Under Cuban constitutional law, sovereignty pertains to the nation, and no ruler is empowered to sign or ratify pacts or treaties that limit or impair national sovereignty or the nation's territorial integrity in any way. At the time the land for the base was leased, the Cuban government was not in fact empowered to cede any part of the country in perpetuity. Moreover, the present constitution of the Republic of Cuba — which was approved by 97.7 percent of the voters in a referendum held on February 24, 1976 — states (chapter 1, paragraph 10) that the Cuban nation repudiates and considers illegal and null and void all treaties, pacts or concessions that are arrived at in conditions of inequality or that relinquish or diminish its sovereignty over any portion of its national territory.

At the age of 19 and as a soldier in the defense of his homeland, Ramón López Peña had hopes of eventually becoming an agricultural machinery mechanic. He probably would have done just that if two US sentries at the Guantánamo Naval Base had not shot him dead. It was after 7:00 p.m. on July 19, 1964. The provocations from the US sentry box had escalated from shouted insults to obscene gestures and stone throwing. The Cuban sentries remained calm, not responding to any of the hostile acts, but suddenly two Marines in the US sentry box threw themselves on the floor and with automatic rifles shot at the Cuban sentry box some meters away.

Ramón was standing guard at the time and was ordered to seek protection in the trench along with his comrades, but another burst of fire mowed him down before he got there. Mortally wounded, he died 20 minutes later. However, Ramón was by no means the first Cuban to be murdered by the US Marines in and from that occupied territory. The history of acts of aggression and provocation centering around the Guantánamo base began as soon as the base was established. Prior to the revolution in

January 1959, such actions were the main expression of the utter scorn the United States had for Cuban rights and its lack of respect for Cuba's national integrity. After 1959, the Guantánamo base became a constant source of friction aimed at providing a pretext for possible US armed intervention in Cuba.

After its 19th-century intervention in Cuba, the United States considered everything to do with the island to be part of US domestic policy. Thus Cuban patriot Juan Gualberto Gómez's words to the constitutional convention at the beginning of this century were prophetic: "The [Platt] Amendment was like giving it [the United States] the key to our house so it could come and go at all hours." And that was just what the United States did until 1959. Cuba was seen as nothing more than the backyard of the Guantánamo base.

In 1912, supported by the Platt Amendment, the troops stationed at the base occupied various parts of the eastern region of the country to crush an armed uprising against the Cuban government—even though the government had not asked them for help. Some years later, in that same part of the island, US troops occupied the railroads when the railway workers called a strike against the US-owned rail company.

On December 17, 1940, a US foreman in charge of work at the base murdered Lino Rodríguez, a Cuban construction worker. Fishermen from Caimanera found his body in the bay with marks of a brutal beating and bullet wounds. The foreman later confessed to the attack but was never duly punished by the US authorities.

In September 1954, a Cuban worker Lorenzo Salomón was arrested and then tortured for two weeks. The US authorities said he had embezzled money, but they never presented any evidence to the Cuban authorities—who were the only ones empowered to take any action. The Cuban government in that period usually displayed a thoroughly servile tolerance of whatever abuses were committed by US personnel. The same tolerance was shown toward the rampages of US Marines and sailors through the Cuban towns, such as Caimanera, the town nearest the base.

Caimanera, with a population of about 8,000 at that time, became a center of prostitution, gambling and drugs serving the US troops. It had over 60 brothels, with around 700 prostitutes. Signs such as "Arizona Bar" and "Marilyn Bar" flanked its long main street. These places were for the enlisted men, while the officers had a more elegant club fronting the town's main square.

The US troops engaged in fights, abuses of all kinds, acts of public aggression and disrespect for the Cuban authorities, who were powerless to establish order, because Cuban laws were not applicable to the Marines and sailors even when they were in Cuban territory.

During the struggle against the regime of General Batista (1952–58) — a de facto government that had first the complicity and then the recognition and support of the United States — the base served as a center supplying fuel and ammunition to the dictatorship's planes that indiscriminately bombed rural areas and defenseless towns. Photographs taken on the base's landing strips while the planes took on those supplies were published in the US press and in newspapers in other parts of the world as irrefutable proof of the support the United States was giving to the Batista regime while the revolutionary forces were fighting in the mountains in the eastern part of the country.

ESCALATION OF INCIDENTS AFTER THE REVOLUTION

The triumph of the Cuban revolution meant an end to the status quo for US geopolitical aspirations in Latin America and the Caribbean. Cuba proved to be an irritating pebble in the shoe of US interests, and US ruling circles immediately unleashed their hostility against the island. The Guantánamo base became a permanent focal point of conflicts.

On January 12, 1961 — just a few days after the United States broke off diplomatic relations with Cuba—Manuel Prieto González, a worker at the base, was arrested, accused of being an agent of the Cuban revolutionary government. He was tortured and forced to swallow pills containing poison. Two months later, early in the morning of March 13, 1961, a pirate boat coming from the base shot at the Santiago de Cuba oil refinery with heavy-caliber machine guns and 57-mm cannon. Cuban sailor René Rodríguez was killed in that attack, which also seriously damaged the plant.

On September 30 of that same year, Rubén López Sabariego, a worker at the base, was arrested by the Military Intelligence Corps. Eighteen days later, a US official notified López Sabariego's wife that his body had been found in a ditch on the base. Medical examination of his body showed that he had been beaten to death. Former Lieutenant William A. Szili of the US navy, one of the accessories to the crime, told a *Philadelphia Bulletin* reporter that Captain Arthur J. Jackson had finished off the Cuban worker with some shots.

Rodolfo Rosell Salas, a fisherman, was kidnapped, tortured and savagely murdered in the US military enclave in May 1962. His mutilated body, bearing stab wounds, was found in his boat, adrift in the bay near Caimanera. On August 23, 1963, the US destroyer *DD 864* ran down the Cuban schooner *Joven Amalia* at the entrance to Guantánamo Bay. Cuban photographer Berto Belén was wounded in the right hand and ear on February 23, 1965, shot while he was preparing to take pictures of an act of provocation and holding his camera at eye level—which showed that the shot was intended to kill.

On numerous occasions US Marines have also shot at the Cuban flag near the northeast gate. In contrast, the Cuban sentries show respect when the US flag is raised or lowered in the same area. US Marines shooting at Cuban sentry boxes killed Ramón López Peña in 1964 and Luis Ramírez López in 1966, both members of the border patrol. In other acts of aggression against Cuban sentry boxes, they wounded soldiers Luis Ramírez Reyes, Antonio Campos and Andrés Noel Larduet.

After López Peña's death, the Cuban government took a series of measures to prevent incidents at the border so the US authorities could not claim that Cuba was the aggressor. Among other things, the Cuban sentry boxes were moved back from the dividing line and fortifications built and a security strip was completed in 1970. This was an important step that required considerable human and material resources. Far from responding positively to Cuba's efforts in this regard, the United States launched a new phase of aggression.

The base also became a reception center for those who, charged with murder and torture, were fleeing from Cuban justice. The US authorities gave asylum to nearly 1,000 known murderers and henchmen of Batista's dictatorship. Some of them were later sent out to infiltrate Cuban territory, carrying out acts of sabotage and organizing armed groups in the nearby mountain areas after US military personnel had given them training on the base.

Between 1959 and 1962, before an effective system of vigilance and defense had been established on the border, the US military enclave was an important center of counterrevolutionary operations that the CIA directed through the Office of Naval Intelligence. Liaison agents with the counterrevolutionary organizations that operated in some parts of Cuban territory were sent out from the base; in particular, weapons and other materiel for insurrectional groups and means for sabotaging the economy were sent into the eastern part of the country, and plans were hatched for assassinating leaders of the revolution.

A revealing example of such deeds was the plan drawn up on the base for mounting an "attack" against itself as a pretext for the United States to intervene militarily in Cuba — a plan that Ernesto Che Guevara denounced in the Inter-American Economic and

Social Council meeting that was held in Punta del Este, Uruguay, in 1961. That plan, called "Immediate Action," which was exposed by individuals who were in contact with the military chief of the base, included an assassination attempt against Raúl Castro during the mass meeting held in Santiago de Cuba, near the base, to celebrate July 26.

"Immediate Action" called for placing no less than four mortars on a farm adjoining the naval base. They were to fire six shells against the US enclave. At the same time, another mortar was to start firing against a nearby artillery emplacement of the Cuban army, so that, believing itself under attack from the base, it would start shooting. Thus, a pretext would be created for US military intervention in Cuba. Captain Caels E. Echemnweiss, who was chief of the base at the time, was one of the most active promoters of the plot, but his view of the plan of action, along with the final decision-making, was in conflict with the CIA project. Subsequent commentaries suggested that this friction led to Captain Echemnweiss being replaced by Admiral Edward J. O'Donnell as commander of the naval base.

Cuban intelligence uncovered the conspiracy. The plotters were arrested, including José Amparo Rosabal, one of the main ringleaders, who had sought refuge in the Guantánamo base after the mercenary invasion at the Bay of Pigs in 1961. When asked about the weapons which were taken from them, Rosabal and his accomplices stated that US troops on the base had given them weapons, which they took into Cuban territory at a point on the border three miles from Boquerón—the same place where, years later, Luis Ramírez López was murdered.

Since 1960, as part of a plan to ease the pressure that militiamen and members of the Rebel Army were exerting against the groups of counterrevolutionaries who had taken up arms in the Escambray—a mountainous area in the middle of the country—the CIA used the base to link similar armed bands in the mountains near Guantánamo and Baracoa. A total of five counterrevolution-ary groups were organized from the base, but they did not survive their first armed actions. Those who were not captured sought refuge in the US military enclave.

The Cuban authorities have also uncovered several conspir-acies organized by agents recruited on the base. When Ricardo Fernández Blanco, one of the ringleaders, was arrested, he con-fessed that he had ties with a Major Morrison of Naval Intelligence. Another captured agent, Cornelio Lewis Philips, a Jamaican employed on the base, said he had been given a CIA course on how to obtain military and economic information and how to provide support for the counterrevolutionary bands in the area. He stated that he reported directly to the admiral in charge of the US military base.

The many hostile acts the US government carried out on the base have also included actions against the Cubans employed in the enclave—including their wholesale firing as a political reprisal. The US military installation had employed thousands of Cubans. When it was fortified and enlarged during World War II, nearly 10,000 Cubans worked on the base. Later, that number dropped to around 6,000. Some of these workers were seasonal workers, while others were permanent.

After the revolution, political tensions and the breaking of diplomatic relations between Cuba and the United States further reduced the Cuban workforce. At the time of the October 1962 Missile Crisis, around 3,500 Cubans still worked at the base, but between February and May of 1964 the US government laid off more than 700 Cuban employees, most of them with more than 20 years' service and unblemished records—as attested to by certificates and diplomas issued by the US authorities themselves.

The workers were given a simple ultimatum: stay on the base and renounce your Cuban citizenship, or go home right now. Choose: inside or out. The US authorities made efforts to persuade some of them, saying that Fidel Castro's government would not stay in power more than a few days. In many cases, the employee was approached at work, told to choose immediately or be put in a vehicle and deposited at the northeast gate.

Six percent of the wages of all those Cuban men and women had been withheld to form a retirement fund — as part of their contracts — but those who opted to leave were never able to draw on it. All are entitled to claim pensions from the US government — a sum that, all told, amounted to over $4 million by the end of 1991.

One of the former base employees, Emilio Samson, was informed by the Office of Personnel Management in Washington, D.C., 25 years after he was thrown off the base, that he had accumulated a little over $36,000. Another, Waldo Limonta, was informed that his pension had been increased by $68 a month from January 1, 1981, to the amount of $780 a month. None of those workers has been able to collect a cent, however, because the economic blockade that the United States has maintained against Cuba for more than 50 years deprives them of access to their funds. The US reply is always the same: it will not give money to "Castro's communist government."

The former Guantánamo workers even presented their case to Javier Pérez de Cuéllar, then secretary-general of the United Nations, and he referred the matter to the UN Human Rights Commission. They also presented it to US Congressman Michael Bilirakis, the commander of the base and the Vatican (through the Papal Nuncio in Havana), with no success to date.

The overwhelming majority of those men and women are now over 60 years old; some have died. The only support they have received came from the government of Cuba, which granted them protection under the social security laws in effect in the country and found jobs for them as soon as they were fired by the US authorities.

From 1962 through April 1992, US personnel carried out 13,255 acts of provocation from the occupied territory—an average of 441.8 a year, 36.8 a month, or 1.2 a day. The most common forms of aggression against the Cuban sentry boxes have been offensive language, obscene gestures or pornographic acts; the throwing of stones and other objects; violations of the dividing line and of Cuba's airspace and territorial waters; rifle and pellet gunshots; and aiming weapons, cannon, tanks and machine guns toward the unoccupied territory.

The acts of provocation have included breaking the fence around the base, climbing the fence, using fire hoses to douse the Cuban side of the line, landing military helicopters in the un-occupied area and using reflectors to illuminate the Cuban sentry boxes. The Cuban government has sent notes to the US government protesting all these acts of provocation and aggression, but, in the vast majority of the cases, it has received no reply in accord with international law.

The international community has been made aware of these constant provocations and of the evidence Cuba has presented to support its protests in many forums, especially the United Nations and the Movement of Nonaligned Countries. Foreign correspondents accredited in Cuba and special envoys from the most diverse media outlets, including those of the United States, have visited the border guarded by the Cuban troops to learn of the violations on the spot and to speak with witnesses.

Cuba has presented evidence of these acts of aggression for more than 30 years and none of the US administrations have been able to deny the charges, for they are irrefutable. At the same time, no one has ever been able to present any proof of violations of the occupied territory of Guantánamo by Cuban border guards.

Luis Ramírez López was the last person shot down by US sentries while on guard duty at the border with the occupied area. His case was the only one which the US authorities, through their State Department, have acknowledged, but, in an attempt to justify the crime, they resorted to obvious lies. The US government stated the Cuban soldier had entered the territory of the base and that a Marine first fired a warning shot to get him to stop and then, when he kept on coming, fired again, killing him.

If Ramírez López had attempted the action attributed to him by the US authorities, he would have had to climb over three fences, each two meters high and topped with a piece of galvanized metal in the form of an "X" with three strands of barbed wire on each of its top pieces, or cut through the heavy wire mesh of those fences with special wire cutters in daylight, in full view of the well-armed Marines who keep close watch on the base's perimeter. Even if he had managed to do that, how could he, mortally wounded and moving through a minefield, once again climb back over the system of fences protecting the Cuban approaches so as to die in his sentry box? The shot that caused his death entered his body at an upward slant. The Cuban sentry box is higher than the place from which the US Marine fired. Moreover, he was shot in the back, yet the US authorities claim he was advancing toward the Marines and was ordered to halt by someone who was ahead of him and who then shot him from the front.

Luis Ramírez López, a 20-year-old farmer, had volunteered for the revolutionary armed forces; he was chosen as a member of the border patrol because of his loyalty to the revolution, his proven bravery and his calm approach to daily life. He had planned to become an engineer.

December 7 is the day on which Cubans honor the men and women who gave their lives in the struggles for Cuba's independence. On that day in 1989, while the bodies of Cubans killed on missions of solidarity in Angola and other parts of the world were being buried, another act of provocation took place. "The guard was changed at 10:02," Lieutenant Luis Rodríguez Fabier, of the border patrol, wrote in the log. At that moment, as he stood in the sentry box of post 17 of the eastern Cuban sector, a bullet fired from just inside the perimeter of the US base missed his forehead by only a few millimeters.

Two hours later, something similar occurred at post 18 in the same sector, very near the place Luis Ramírez López had been murdered. José Angel Castillo, who was standing guard at the time, told the Cuban and foreign press that he was walking along the balcony of the sentry box, observing his designated area, when he suddenly heard the glass in the front window of the sentry box shatter a few centimeters behind him, at head level. When he turned around, he saw a bullet hole. Ballistics experts who were consulted said the two bullets came from a special rifle used by a sharpshooter who fired against both Cuban sentry boxes from near post 13 on the US side. Ten minutes after the second shot, a white pickup truck, presumably belonging to the intelligence service on the base, picked up an individual carrying a rifle who was around 1,500 meters away from the second Cuban post that had been hit.

There is only one obvious guilty party: the US government. There is only one motive: its limitless hostility to the Cuban revolution. Thus, the Guantánamo base continues to be a powder keg.

GUNBOATS AGAIN

Current US policy on Cuba seems to reflect the boom in remakes of old US movies. Far from changing with the times and expressing its proverbial pragmatism, the US policy of force against its closest neighbor in the Antilles seems to take us back to the days of silent films and the "Big Stick," reinstating gunboats—now in the form of aircraft carriers and missile-carrying cruisers—as floating embassies. The Guantánamo Naval Base has become the stage for this second-rate drama, successfully fulfilling the mission of maintaining and increasing tension between the two nations.

It could well be said that there is an escalation along the border which implies even greater danger, since it involves complex acts of provocation on an increased scale that have been meticulously planned and have clear consequences. Events in the US military enclave in recent decades bear this out.

After the September 1991 coup that deposed the constitutional president of Haiti, Jean-Bertrand Aristide, battle troops and materiel were increased at the base under the pretext of evacuating US citizens from that country. In November of that year, a White House spokesman announced the sending of more Marines to put up around 10,000 tents for Haitian refugees and maintain order in the enclave. In fact, this "humanitarian" act was used to cover up something entirely different.

In a short period of time, over 300 transport planes of different kinds landed at the Guantánamo base, bringing in the men of Joint Task Force 20. They were to take part in Operation Safe Harbor, to be held with the participation of army, Marine and air force units, plus elite and special units, such as the 10th Mountain Light Infantry Division and the 10th Artillery Regiment of the Marines' 2nd Division. The US government sent in the strongest vigilance and protection body ever seen at the base: a police contingent complete with artillery. Did it mobilize such a contingent during the 1992 riots in Los Angeles? Was it preparing to intervene militarily in Haiti, or to stage a large-scale act of provocation against Cuba that would lead to an invasion? A few days later, the forces that had just arrived at the base began a military exercise that lasted for several days and clearly demonstrated one of the US authorities' real intentions.

The exercise simulated the massive entry of Cuban civilians opposed to the revolution at different points along the border, including a dry run of the evacuation of non-military US personnel and foreigners living on the base. The irresponsible, criminal nature of the exercise was exposed when the radio station in the enclave—which can be heard nearby—stated that the evacuation exercise would include many Cubans. This gave the green light to those Cubans wishing to leave illegally, for it implied that those listening to the call should engage in the extremely dangerous action of challenging the strong system of security established in both directions — which includes one of the densest minefields in the world.

The exercise showed that the US government contemplated this variant in its anti-Cuban plans under the heading "humanitarian intervention," as a response to a hypothetical civil war in Cuba. The White House, which is so ready to talk about human rights — although always with its own interpretation — thus endangered the lives of thousands of Cuban citizens to suit US political interests.

Such an action could serve as a catalyst for another large-scale action that, in its various phases, could provide grist for the mill of a campaign on supposed human rights violations in Cuba and could lead to a direct aggressive response by the United States.

Prior to the maneuver and as an indispensable complement to it, diverse media in the United States — especially in Florida — "revealed" false accounts of measures the Cuban government was supposed to have taken for deactivating the minefields and taking down the fences just outside the base so as to permit the massive exodus of those Cubans who had not obtained visas for going to the United States — visas denied by the same government that, from its radio station inside the base, was instigating illegal departures. Among other lies, the mass media spread stories of a supposed attack by a Cuban navy patrol launch against a US fishing vessel and supported the idea of a probable attack by the Cuban air force against the Turkey Point nuclear power plant in Florida.

As if this were not enough, other serious incidents were noted during the exercise, including artillery target practice carried out around 400 meters from the boundary fence with Cuban territory, in the northeast gate sector, instead of at the artillery proving ground inside the base. On that occasion, over 500 shots were recorded, with some of the shells landing near the boundary of the US military installation, which could have had serious consequences. This was one of the most dangerous acts of provocation in recent times.

In other incidents, TA-4J planes permanently based at Guantánamo and a CH-53E helicopter from the reinforcement units have violated Cuban airspace—the planes on five occasions and the helicopter once. The aircraft were carrying their normal weapons when they overflew the Cuban troops' positions, and the helicopter also carried personnel who had engaged in landing exercises inside the base. CH-53E helicopters and C-130 transport planes have also practiced air landing techniques both by day and night.

The US naval presence in the bay has been increased; at moments of maximum tension, over 20 warships, including five missile-carrying cruisers, a submarine and the helicopter carrier *Guam*, have been anchored there. Moreover, NATO ships have entered the bay to offload supplies. In the same period, a naval group composed of six amphibious craft headed by an LPH-12 helicopter carrier with the capacity to disembark a reinforced battalion of Marines was also in the area.

A high-ranking Marine officer explained the exercises on the base by saying that troop training should be carried out in conditions closely resembling those of the place of possible combat, so what could be better than Guantánamo, right on the spot? Well-informed sources say that this has become standard operating procedure of the US Army in recent times, and maneuvers are carried out in tropical areas very similar to Cuba.

In the exercises, the "adversaries" are units that have studied what weapons and abilities the Cuban units have and assume their structure and composition. For example, units of the 101st Airborne Division, part of the rapid deployment forces, engaged in such actions in the practice maneuvers carried out at the Fort

Chaffee, Arkansas, battle training center in September and October 1991. The same thing has happened, using different US units, at other training centers, such as the one at Fort Irwin, where an "adversary" group called the Atlantics assumes the properties of Cuban troops. Moreover, the commentary accompanying these actions, as provided by General Colin Powell, then chairman of the Joint Chiefs of Staff, and one of the most outspoken of Cuba's opponents, is on a par with the rest of the campaign.

In an interview published in the April 15, 1991, issue of *Navy Times*, General Powell said, "I'm running out of demons. I'm running out of villains. I'm down to Castro and Kim Il Sung." He was even more explicit on arriving at the Guantánamo base—he was the highest ranking military officer to visit it since the October 1962 Missile Crisis—on January 6, 1992.

On that occasion, he said that danger still existed in the world, which is why the United States had 1,700 young men and women in places such as Guantánamo, because they had a mission to fulfill there. The Vietnam veteran's words represent more than an isolated, hasty comment triggered by circumstance and typify a mentality shaped by other war frustrations; they form a doctrinaire concept that is prevalent at the highest levels of the US military hierarchy.

The Joint Chiefs of Staff decision to open a special office for monitoring the Cuban situation—an office headed by Frank Libutti, coordinator of the Cuba group, who was General Powell's immediate subordinate—is more proof of that line of thinking. In addition, high-ranking US military officers have appeared before the Armed Services Committees of the Senate and House to set forth their ideas on a probable social outburst in Cuba and a massive, disorderly emigration of Cubans to the US base which could endanger "the national security of the United States." General James Clapper, chief of military intelligence, told the members of the Senate Armed Services Committee on January

22, 1992, that the Cuban situation had reached such a point that it could cause problems for the national security of the United States. He said he based his analysis on the rapid deterioration of the Cuban economy, which could quickly lead to generalized violence and a massive, disorderly exodus to the United States by sea or to the Guantánamo installation, among other possibilities.

Admiral Leon A. Edney, chief of the Atlantic Command, told the members of the same committee on March 4, 1992, that Cuba posed the greatest threat to the security of the United States in the Atlantic, for the same reasons given by General Clapper. He emphasized that his command was keeping very close tabs on the situation and was preparing to meet any eventuality.

A few weeks earlier, the February 18 issue of the *International Herald Tribune* contained a summary of a 70-page report drawn up by a group of Pentagon experts headed by an admiral who was also deputy chairman of the Joint Chiefs of Staff; it described the theaters of operations for armed conflicts that the United States would probably wage in the coming period. One of those seven places was the Caribbean—including, of course, Cuba.

This line of thinking in top US military circles was given more publicity when an article on the Pentagon's draft strategic plan—directed by then Undersecretary of Defense Paul D. Wolfowitz—appeared in the *New York Times* on March 8, 1992. It described the supposed internal crisis in Cuba, saying that it implied new challenges for the United States and that, therefore, it was necessary to have a contingency plan for handling everything from a massive exodus of Cubans to the United States to a military provocation by Cuba against the United States or any of its allies, to a war on the island.

One may well ask why the supreme command of the Armed Forces of the United States suddenly became so interested in Guantánamo—something that had not ever happened before in the long history of that enclave. High-ranking US military brass have visited Guantánamo more than 40 times, but the two visits that General Colin Powell made to the base in the first three months of 1992 and the five visits by Admiral Edney, chief of the Atlantic Command, to cite two examples, were particularly notable. Moreover, the head of the United States Interests Section in Cuba visited Guantánamo, too.

Another expression of the US authorities' hostility toward Cuba was the Ocean Venture '92 exercise, held in areas very close to the island, including the Guantánamo Naval Base, with participation by over 30,000 members of the US elite forces, and dozens of warships and planes. Such exercises are carried out on a regular basis, but this was more threatening than others because of the US government's intensification of its aggressive policy against Cuba.

The composition of the participating forces, their goal and the main center of action clearly showed against whom the staff of the 18th Airborne Army Corps, the members of the 82nd and 101st Airborne Divisions, the 24th Armored Division, the 10th Mountain Light Infantry Division, the 2nd Marine Expeditionary Force and the Special Operations Forces—all with special previous training on the scene of a probable military intervention against Cuba— were directing their preparations.

Together with those units, more than 20 warships of different kinds from the Atlantic Fleet, including the commands of two aircraft carrier battle groups and aircraft of the 12th Air Force, also participated in the exercise. US military spokespeople had already told the press that the public objectives of the maneuver were to train and check the capacities of a joint force protecting the national interests of the United States and of military support for its allies in the area of responsibility of the Atlantic Command.

US taxpayers should ask themselves why, when all are feeling pinched by the economic recession and their own government says the Cold War and the East-West conflict are over, they should pay for those exercises. Moreover, elementary logic shows that a small, poor country such as Cuba cannot pose the slightest threat to the most powerful nation in the world.

All this shows the furious hostility against Cuba that has prevailed in US policy, bent on stepping up the tension that has existed for so long between the two countries. During the Reagan and Bush years, an imperial atmosphere reigned in the White House, with mistaken, dangerous boasting to the effect that the only enemy left for the United States was "red Cuba."

BEDROCK ARROGANCE

Crushing the Cuban revolution has been a frustrated presidential obsession ever since the Eisenhower administration, for both Republicans and Democrats. In more than 10 consecutive administrations, this policy has been a stubbornly recurring theme, sustained by force and an ideology of sorts. It is also obvious that the belligerent US policy against Cuba in no way reflects a coherent approach to its international relations.

President George H. Bush, for example, defended relations with the People's Republic of China—a nation his administration has accused of having committed serious human rights violations—pointing out that it is better to maintain relations with a transgressing nation in order to influence it and bring it into line. In his time, Ronald Reagan did the same concerning South Africa with his "constructive compromise."

It is said in the United States that the Cold War ended with the collapse of European socialism and the disintegration of the Soviet Union. How, then, can the US government explain its obsessive interest in destroying the Cuban revolution?

These days the White House has no basis for its main arguments against Cuba, such as the "Soviet threat" from Cuba or the revolution's willingness to support the national liberation movements in Latin America or elsewhere. In 1987 and 1988, the

Cuban government freed most of the prisoners who were serving sentences for having committed crimes against the government; in that same period, it allowed human rights groups to visit jails and talk with prisoners.

By virtue of the sovereign decision of Cuba and Angola, Cuban troops were withdrawn from Angola. Yet in May 1989, shortly after the signing of those agreements, then US Secretary of State James Baker made public a memorandum in which he declared that an easing of Cuba-US relations was not possible because, for years, Cuba's conduct had not changed in any way to justify such a position.

The White House reacted like an ostrich, sticking its head in the sand and refusing to face reality. Moreover, when all other arguments were exhausted, it resorted to its old arsenal and stepped up its activities in Guantánamo to provoke a conflict that could unleash larger, devastating actions; it also increased its military presence in the area with exercises such as Ocean Venture. High-ranking government officials, however, declared that the United States had no intention of attacking Cuba. Robert Gelbard, for example, reiterated the [first] Bush administration's position when addressing the House Committee on Foreign Affairs in late 1991.

His apparently pro-peace statement was aimed at calming sectors of world public opinion that no longer accepted the argument that Cuba was a Soviet military springboard for attacking the United States. It was also directed at the US people, since more and more of them fail to view their tiny neighbor as a terrifying version of the "Evil Empire," as Reagan described the Soviet Union. And many even want relations between the two countries to be normalized — as shown in the latest polls.

Once again, the words of the United States were one thing, and its deeds, another, for the evidence of hostility continued. For example, 523 military reconnaissance flights were carried out against Cuba between January 1, 1989, and December 31, 1991. In that same period, US tactical planes based in Florida made more than 80,000 flights to within 100 kilometers of western Cuba, where Havana is located—that is, seven or eight minutes' flying time away for a combat plane.

Most recently, the US Air Force has also intensified its exercises in areas near the island, with strong naval groups, including the battle groups of the aircraft carriers CV-66 *America* and CV-60 *Saratoga*. In addition to these military contingents, ships, planes, radar and other types of sensing devices in the region (supposedly there to combat drug trafficking) engage in constant reconnaissance. An average of 10 to 15 ships and 20 to 25 planes take part in those activities every day.

Cuba is in a difficult situation, for it has lost the support of its allies, the former Soviet Union and other formerly socialist countries. The US response—not only opportunistic but criminal—was to tighten the blockade in an attempt to strangle the Cuban revolution. Its refusal to allow ships from third countries that have touched Cuban ports to enter US ports is an example of this. The Torricelli act, which banned trade with Cuba by US subsidiaries in other nations—an act that undermined those nations' sovereignty and also constituted a restriction on free trade—was narrowly adopted by the US Congress in 1992.

The US policy of unrelenting hostility to Cuba has failed to bear fruit after more than five decades, even though it has created many problems for Cuba. Therefore, it would be only logical to take a realistic or pragmatic line; in fact, however, the US authorities seem bent on demonstrating the truth of the old refrain that common sense is the least common of our senses.

The United States is not going to give up its dreams of destroying the Cuban revolution, but it can choose between two paths: that of hostility and aggression or that of peace—by which it could try to influence political affairs on the island through other means. The first alternative has proven to be totally ineffective, although the United States has not yet resorted to military intervention, which would inevitably lead to another Vietnam.

It has not tried the second alternative. As a matter of principle, Cuba is not opposed to a policy of peaceful coexistence, and Fidel Castro has stated that, if the US authorities lift the economic blockade and stop their threats, campaigns and war against Cuba, another form of political leadership in the country could be considered, both in theory and in practice.

Cuba has shown that it can stand firm and knows that its goals are realistic. It is struggling to create an equitable society that meets the people's needs, without clinging to old, foreign models. Because its revolution is of, by and for its people, Cuba is free of the serious ills that led to the demise of European socialism.

When the United States examines its differences with Cuba, it should dig down to the core, to the essence of the problem. It has tried to show that communism is to blame, but this is not the case. The United States has been set on annexing Cuba come hell or high water since long before the doctrine of communism was formulated, long before the Bolshevik revolution of 1917, and long before Fidel Castro led the popular victory over the US-backed Batista dictatorship. Rather, what lies at the heart of this dispute is the US authorities' resistance to seeing Cuba become a free and sovereign nation.

The Guantánamo base is the concentrated expression of those unsatisfied geopolitical ambitions and the arrogance of the powerful when faced with something that did not turn out the way they wanted. Calm, realistic reflection is worth much more than positions of irrationality and force. Those who govern the United States perhaps should go back—with the humility and greatness of the founding fathers of their nation—to the origins of their homeland and, out of love and respect for their history and for the US citizens they represent, apply the principle of the natural right of every people to determine its own destiny for itself.

REFERENCES

Archives of the Revolutionary Armed Forces. Border Patrol. Museum of History

Benítez, José A., "200 años de codicia, hostilidad y agresiones," *Granma*, Havana, May 28, 1980.

D'Estéfano Pisani, Miguel A, *Cuba, Estados Unidos y el Derecho Internacional Contemporáneo*, (Havana: Ed. Ciencias Sociales, 1983).

Film and video archives of the Revolutionary Armed Forces Movie and Television Studios (ECITVFAR).

Foner, Phillip S., *Historia de Cuba y sus relaciones con Estados Unidos*, (Havana: Ed. Ciencias Sociales, 1973).

Gómez, Máximo, "En una guerra un hombre es un número, la idea lo es todo," in *La Nación Cubana*, No 9, Vol. 3, (Havana: 1983).

"Que prepara Estados Unidos en Guantánamo," en *Granma,* May 5, 1992.

Toste Ballart, Gilberto, *Guantánamo: USA al desnudo*, (Havana: Editora Política, 1990).

Yglesia Martínez, Teresita, *Cuba, primera república, segunda ocupación*, (Havana: Ed. Ciencias Sociales, 1976)

HOW TO END THE GUANTÁNAMO TREATY

Olga Miranda

LEGAL CONSIDERATIONS ON THE TERMINATION OF THE GUANTÁNAMO TREATY

Whenever I used to discuss the issue of the naval base at Guantánamo, I was asked if it was true that the United States would leave in the year 2002, that is to say, 99 years from 1903. When I answered that perhaps on that date they would no longer need the base, the question about the termination of the 1903 and 1934 treaties—or rather, the illegal occupation—inevitably cropped up.

Sooner or later, the United States must dismantle the base and return its territory to Cuba, but that will require good faith from the occupier and their attention to the demands of the Cuban people and the opinion of the international community, as expressed as long ago as the 1964 conference of the Movement of Nonaligned Countries held in Cairo.

The conference considered that the maintenance by the United States of the naval base at Guantánamo, against the will of the Cuban government and people—and despite the provisos in the declaration of the 1961 Belgrade conference—is a violation of Cuba's sovereignty and territorial integrity. The Cairo conference also noted that the Cuban government had stated its willingness to resolve its dispute with the US government regarding the military base at Guantánamo on an equal footing. Therefore, the Cairo conference requested that the US government hold negotiations with the government of Cuba to withdraw from that military facility.

To speculate, I think that the end of the US occupation of Guantánamo could happen in three different ways:

- With the voluntary abandonment of the base by the United States (unilateral action).
- Through negotiation between Cuba and the United States (bilateral action).
- With the presentation of the case before the International Court of Justice (multilateral action).

My references to early treaties concerning the base, such as the Agreement on Coaling and Naval Stations, the Complementary Agreement and the Platt Amendment, are made with the idea of informing readers about the legal background of the base. According to statements made by the United States, in a legal confrontation over the issue of the base the US argument would focus primarily on the 1934 treaty. That would be their mistake — the 1934 treaty refers back to the 1903 agreement, raising the issue of Cuba's lack of freedom of consent in making the agreement, faced as it was with coercion, blackmail and the implied threat of force.

The termination of a treaty requires, in the first place, the application of the terms of the treaty itself, and, therefore, each of the elements of the treaty must be examined. I will now approach in detail the two ways that the 1934 treaty allows for its termination, and I will refer later to a third option.

UNILATERAL ACTION

"For the time required" and "so long as the United States of America shall not abandon [it]" are phrases from the February 16/23, 1903, and May 29, 1934, treaties between Cuba and the United States. According to the latter document, one of the ways that the leasing rights of the United States could be repealed is if *ex proprio motu*, of its own free will, that nation voluntarily left the base.

To date, there has been no hint that the United States is thinking about leaving the base at Guantánamo; consequently, it is not worthwhile to speculate about this. Besides, this solution is out of our hands. It would only require the United States to dismantle the base and withdraw from the occupied territory. That would be the most sensible action.

BILATERAL ACTION

Another possibility for terminating the lease of the Guantánamo base is expressed in the 1934 treaty, where in the beginning of Article III reads: "Until the two contracting parties agree to the modification of the [February 1903] agreement."

The idea expressed in this sentence does not really imply the termination of the occupation of the territory—it indicates more the US desire to maintain the possibility of implementing later a new, more modern form of agreement, like the treaties they have signed since 1940 to legitimize their military bases in foreign territories.

The idea of abandoning the base, that is to say, the unilateral action mentioned in the 1903 agreements and ratified in the 1934 treaty, is the one that survives in the sentence, "as long as the United States of America shall not abandon the naval base at Guantánamo." For that reason, it would be worthwhile to explain here that when the 1934 treaty is mentioned, the treatment of the base in the 1903 agreement is implicit. Thus, it would not be absurd to speak about the "1903/1934 treaty or agreement."

The 1969 Vienna Convention on the Law of Treaties establishes that a state may not contend a cause to annul or terminate a treaty if, after knowing about a violation, it has expressly communicated that:

- The treaty is valid, or;
- It is still in effect, or;
- Its application continues, or;
- It has been verified in such a way that it must be deemed to have acquiesced to the validity of the treaty or to its continued enforcement or application, according to the case in question.

I ask myself if the United States could at some point claim the continuity of the application of the treaty on the base due to the simple fact that its troops remain in it, notwithstanding the coercion and threats and violations of the treaty by the US side. I also ask myself whether that undesired permanence could signify Cuba's acquiescence and, consequently, a sort of validation that negates the demand that the treaty be annulled due to the element of duress in the agreement. However, it is publicly and well known that the Cuban people never consented to the US presence imposed upon them, moreover the agreement was a violation of the Cuban constitution that was rejected by a popular referendum which also declared the agreement unlawful and invalid.

A grave violation—understood as the violation of an essential term of the treaty—and also a fundamental change of circumstances (*rebus sic stantibus*) that radically modifies the scope of the treaty can cause the termination of a treaty.

The Helms-Burton law of March 1996, a monstrosity created by the United States that meddles in everything "human and divine" regarding Cuba, predetermines when the issue of the Guantánamo

Naval Base can be addressed by the government of the United States with the government of Cuba; and consequently, with the Helms-Burton law the United States has unilaterally modified the 1903/1934 treaty that they themselves state is in effect.

Let us recall that the treaty leaves the termination of the lease to the will of the United States: "for the time required." Now, thanks to Section 201 (12) of Chapter II of the Helms-Burton law, the government of the United States is required to be "ready to begin negotiations" with a Cuban government of which they approved, that is, that fitted their "democratic" pattern. The requirement in the treaty that the base be held only while it is useful has been made irrelevant since March 1996, when the Helms-Burton law was implemented. The duration of the base will now depend on whether Cuba has a government that Washington approves of.

Therefore, because of the Helms-Burton law — an imperial instrument that prevails over the so-called treaty, created with a unilateral decision taken by one of the two parties — although the base may become an annoyance (as, in fact, it is), and although US taxpayers must continue to pay for the mess created by the Helms-Burton law in general and particularly to keep the naval base at Guantánamo, the hands of the US government will be tied to the implementation of the existing treaty.

The Helms-Burton law ruling is further proof that the continued existence of the naval base in Guantánamo is imposed on Cuba by the United States with no legal backing whatsoever and without consideration for the will of the Cuban people. From the beginning, the naval base was a unilateral creation of the United States, and the latest act confirms this once again.

The sponsors of the Helms-Burton law, who, in a shameless and indecent fashion purport to turn Cuba into a protectorate, to make the republic disappear, to annex it to the federation of the stars and stripes, should remember the words of José Martí: "Cubans, sometimes indomitable by dint of rebelliousness, are as harsh toward despotism as they are courteous toward reason. Cubans are independent, moderate and proud. They are their own masters and they want no other masters. Whoever intends to saddle them will be shaken off."

MULTILATERAL ACTION

According to Article 35 of the statutes of the International Court of Justice, the court is open to all party states and, according to Article 92 of the UN Charter, all members of the organization are, *ipso facto*, parties to the statutes of the court. As a member of the United Nations and consequently as a party to the court, Cuba can present its demands before the court. However, to present a case it must first be decided that the court is competent. Cuba has stated that it does not accept the compulsory jurisdiction of the court. Consequently, in order to take a case before the court, both Cuba and the United States have to be in agreement, while at this time neither of the two states accepts the obligation of submitting their disputes for resolution at the International Court of Justice.

According to Article 38 of the court's statutes, if the state against which a request is made has not accepted the controversy presented before the court by the plaintiff state, the request or demand will not be registered, and no procedure will be initiated until the state against which the request was made accepts the competence of the court in regard to the issue in question. However, the court will make that request known to the defendant state. The court's competence in regard to contentious issues depends on the litigating states accepting the initiation of the process.

Another important question is the nature of the dispute, which has to be legal rather than political. Only in exceptional cases have political disputes been accepted, when they endanger international peace and security. The plaintiff state must establish the court's competence and the fact that there exists a dispute of a legal character. Due to the fact that neither Cuba nor the United States acknowledge the obligatory competence of the court, they will have to reach a prior agreement to accept that it is competent in this regard.

I have referred to some primary issues regarding the basic procedure before the court, without delving further into this question. To take a bilateral dispute before the court, both parties have to agree to submit to its jurisdiction, and it must be proved that all other peaceful means to solve the controversy — especially negotiations, mediation, conciliation, etc. — have been tried without success.

In repeated statements by the Cuban government regarding treaties that invoke the International Court of Justice as the solution to controversies stemming from them, our country has made clear its preference for a solution by means of negotiations, and has not accepted the compulsive application of the jurisdiction of the court.

The Cuban stance on the compulsory statute of the court is based on the court's controversial performance in cases concerning the interests of underdeveloped countries.

The court's only significant ruling came on June 27, 1986, when it declared US aggression against Nicaragua illegal. The favorable ruling to Nicaragua resulted in the United States retiring from the court, as well as disregarding the adverse ruling in its usual arrogant manner.

The court can also advise about any legal issue at the behest, for example, of the Security Council or the UN General Assembly, but such rulings are not mandatory.

CAUTION AND THOUGHTFULNESS

The Guantánamo Naval Base is not a thing of the past, but of the present and the future; therefore, the interpretation of the possible application of international principles to the termination of the treaty on the base must be done with caution and thoughtfulness. To choose between the peaceful and military options to solve the case of the Guantánamo base demands a high dose of discernment and caution, for the concerned parties may not be the only ones to be directly involved. Such thorny issues as aggression against a small country by a more powerful one do not require philosophizing or theorizing; rather an in-depth analysis of the complete situation and its consequences are the best way to face such issues.

Cubans have been wise enough to pose the Guantánamo issue to themselves as part of a conflict with the United States that must be resolved without resorting to the *ultima ratio*, that is to say, to bellicose actions typical of monarchs and empires. A military attempt to bring about the return of the occupied territory to the people of Cuba would entail grave consequences for the international community.

As I have mentioned, Cuba has not ratified the 1969 Vienna Convention on the Law of Treaties, but given that the existence of treaties without a date of expiry is dealt with by the convention, I think that it would be interesting to make some remarks in that regard. It is a legal norm that treaties without a date of expiry are terminated according to their provisions, or at any time with the consent of the parties involved, as is expressed in Article 54 of the Vienna Convention.

Article 56 of the convention addresses the repudiation of a treaty lacking provisions for its termination. It is a *sine qua non* [mandatory] requisite for the repudiation or withdrawal from such treaties that it is established that it was the intention of the parties concerned to admit the possibility of a withdrawal, or that the right to repudiate or withdraw from the treaty may be inferred from the nature of the treaty itself.

The 1934 treaty does not allow the possibility of a repudiation by the Cuban side, for the expiry of the treaty is in the hands of the other party concerned ("for the time required").

According to some commentators, the issue of the Guantánamo base should be dealt with by the international community. Austrian lawyer Christoph Schreuer has stated: "The case of the naval base at Guantánamo has become increasingly thorny and virulent given the time elapsed and the fact that international law and the community of nations have not played the role that befits them."[1]

Arthur March also refers to the issue of the base in his work *La Science Moderne et ses Theories*, where he remarks: "Our modernity seems powerless to solve some grave problems of international public law, and we are astonished by unquestionable truths that only need a little good faith and a sense of classical justice to be solved, as is the case of the naval base at Guantánamo in Cuba."[2]

I also call attention to the opinion of the US expert David Cavers, a professor at Harvard University, who said the following about the occupation by his country of a portion of Cuba's territory: "Only the cases worsened by time, without an apparent solution, like the case of the naval base at Guantánamo, in which the interest of the international community is involved, acquire certain diffusion when it seems that the injustice of those who for decades have not understood is going to explode, and now no one wants to face and solve once and for all the pending disputes."[3]

The Ecuadorean lawyer Reinaldo Valarezo states in regard to the case: "If international legal norms are left aside, there will be no hope of solving this conflict before this century ends, and the way will not be paved for future applications in other fields of litigation."[4]

The US expert Jan K. Black also refers to the issue of Guantánamo, and offers this valuable opinion: "The solutions for the case of the naval base at Guantánamo within the framework of international law have to be valid at present and not be seen as something to be solved in the future."[5]

It sometimes happens that a theory that may be valid to solve a conflict at a given moment becomes obsolete, or that its application to a seemingly similar case can be completely inadequate. Analogy is worthless in international law, and so are formulas. Guantánamo is a very specific case.

Although many countries have made statements in support of Cuba in its just demand to recover the strip of land snatched away by imperial greed, the idea of international participation has not yet arisen in regard to the conflict over the Guantánamo base. Whether we like it or not, we are all affected by issues of sovereignty and territorial integrity — consequently these principles are fundamental concerns of the United Nations. A *laissez-faire* stance is therefore out of the question.

Cuba and its people have received not only the support and the solidarity of various governments and international organizations, but also of figures who, as individuals, have asked the US government to return the usurped territory occupied by the Guantánamo Naval Base to its legitimate owner. Such is the case of the letters dated July 12, 1996, sent by Guillermo Torriello)former Guatemalan minister of foreign affairs and representative of his country at the foundation of the United Nations, signatory of the San Francisco Charter in 1945, and chairman of Our America's Anti-Imperialist Tribunal) to US Secretary of State Warren Christopher, and to the heads of states and governments who participated in the Third Ibero-American Summit held in San Salvador de Bahía, in Brazil, on July 15–16, 1993.

CLAIM OVER THE OCCUPIED TERRITORY— SOVEREIGN WILL AND THE DECISION OF THE CUBAN PEOPLE

After the Cuban people attained their true independence and full sovereignty with the revolution of January 1, 1959, they continued to bravely demand the return of the portion of their territory usurped by the United States.

However, at a very complex time in the relations between the United States and Cuba, when it was known—as was later proven with the release of declassified documents by the Pentagon—that the United States was concocting a "self-aggression," ie, a fake Cuban aggression against the base, in order to have an excuse to openly attack Cuba, the revolutionary government clearly stated that Cuba would never attack the base. Thus, Fidel Castro said during the Labor Day commemoration held in Havana, on May 1, 1964:

> There are other, older problems, like the problem of the base. The base was there when the revolution triumphed, it is an old problem from half a century ago; we have stated here what our position is regarding the problem of the base, we have stated that we will never resort to force to solve the problem of the base, and that has always been the position of the revolutionary government. Because we know those shameless imperialists, we have followed the policy of not giving them any pretext for their plans. The problem of the base is an old problem, and we can take whatever time is necessary to discuss and resolve it; because it is a problem, an old evil that the revolution found when it came to power...[6]

The Cuban people rejected the unlawful occupation of our territory in Guantánamo by the United States, and it was thus proven when 97.7 percent of Cuban voters approved the 1976 Constitution, in which Article 10 (Article 12 of the modified 1992 Constitution) states: "The Republic of Cuba repudiates and considers illegal and null the treaties, pacts or concessions agreed upon in unequal terms that ignore or diminish its sovereignty over any possession of the national territory."

Thus, the Cuban people ratified their original repudiation of the treaties concerning the Guantánamo base, and consequently the United States must leave that territory unlawfully occupied against the will of the Cuban people.

Raúl Castro, in an interview granted to the newspaper *El Sol de México*, repeated the cautious and wise policy of the revolutionary government in regard to the Guantánamo base:

> We will not act irresponsibly on this matter, but we will not give up our absolutely firm stance demanding our sovereign right over that piece of our country's soil.
>
> As I recently said at the city of Guantánamo, a few kilometers away from the US facility, to us the US military base is a dagger stuck in the side of our homeland. And we intend to draw it out peacefully and in a civilized manner. The demand for the return of the territory of the base is not only Cuba's unanimous claim, but also a clamor of world public opinion.[7]

It is difficult to summarize in a few pages the violations, aggressions and punitive behavior that dagger stuck in our homeland's soil entailed and still entails. But in order to focus readers' minds what I have been saying in the previous pages, I can emphasize the following:

- It is well known that the February 16/23, 1903 agreement and its July 2, 1903, Complementary Agreement, as well as the sequel of those two documents, the May 29, 1934 treaty, concerning the occupation by the United States of land and water at Guantánamo bay and its periphery, where the Guantánamo Naval Base stands, has been and is repudiated — in relation to its origin, manner and maintenance — by the people of Cuba.

- The United States violated their own obligations — stemming from the Joint Resolution dated April 19, 1898, and contracted in the Treaty of Paris, dated December 10, 1898 — by imposing upon the people of Cuba, by coercion and against their will, at a time when Cuba was militarily occupied by US troops, a unilateral resolution approved by the US Congress (the Platt Amendment), a foreign law that allowed the United States the right to occupy certain sites of Cuba's national territory for coaling or naval stations.

- The United States violated the principles consecrated by international law that require all international negotiations to be conducted on equal footing, in good faith, by means of the expression of the parties' free consent to obligate themselves, and that require each party to respect and observe what was agreed upon. In fact, the United States, in regard to the Platt Amendment and to the Permanent Treaty of Relations dated May 22, 1903, [which bound Cuba to the terms of the Platt Amendent], the Agreement on Coaling and Naval Stations of February 16/23, 1903, and its Complementary Agreement of July 2, 1903, coerced the government of Cuba by threatening to use force in all its guises — military, political and economic — to impose upon it those same agreements.

- The United States profoundly and repeatedly violated the cause and object of the Permanent Treaty of Relations (May 22, 1903), the February 16/23, 1903 Agreement, its Complementary Agreement (July 2, 1903) and the Treaty of Relations (May 29, 1934).

- The Cuban people hold full sovereignty over Cuba and the Cuban state holds an inalienable right to the integrity of its territory.

- The people and the government of Cuba have taken a firm position to avoid provocations that may endanger international peace and security, and have warned the United States not to overstep their mark, because they know that the military presence stems from a political decision, and from imperialist arrogance in not complying with our people's legitimate demands.

- International solidarity with the just demands of the Cuban people that the piece of its territory unlawfully occupied by the United States be returned strengthens our cause. Cuba has not been alone, and will not be alone in this struggle; its courage goes hand in hand with the solidarity of the best of humankind.

- Since the triumph of the Cuban revolution, the people of Cuba have reiterated and continue to reiterate their irrevocable right to vindicate the usurped territory, and have demanded and still demand that the US government adopt all necessary measures to effectively vacate the portion of Cuban territory it unlawfully occupies in Guantánamo, leaving it to the free and absolute use and benefit of the Republic of Cuba.

And we can also tell the United States in its own language, so it is clearly understood: *Yankee, go home!* Thus the United States can get rid of the burden of the infamy it shouldered when it imposed upon us the occupation of our territory, where its unwanted naval base now stands.

NOTES

1. Christoph Schreuer, *Die Internationalen Organizationen*, (Salzburg: Salzburg University Press, 1989), 154. Quoted in Nicolaus Keller, *Deliberaciones jurídicas internacionales sobre la Base Naval de Guantánamo en Cuba*, (1995), 24.

2. Arthur March, *La Science Moderne et ses Theories*, (Paris: Editorial Gallimart, 1955), 338–40.

3. David Cavers, *The Choice of Law Process*. Speech delivered at his investiture as Professor Emeritus at Harvard University, (Cambridge: Harvard University Press, 1966). Quoted in Nicolaus Keller, op. cit., 29.

4. Reinaldo Valarezo García, *Manual de derecho internacional*, (Loja: Universidad Nacional de Loja, 1984), 13.

5. Jan K. Black, *Area Handbook for Cuba* (2nd Edition), (Washington D.C.: US Government Printing Office), 352.

6. Fidel Castro Ruz, "Discurso conmemorativo por el Primero de Mayo, La Habana, 1964," in *Política exterior del Gobierno Revolucionario de Cuba, 1959– julio de 1964*, B-5.

7. Raúl Castro Ruz, "Entrevista concedida al periódico *El Sol de México*," in *Bohemia* (Havana: 14 May, 1993) 24.

DOCUMENTS

DOCUMENT 1

THE BRECKENRIDGE MEMORANDUM

On December 24, 1897, J.C. Breckenridge, US undersecretary of war, sent a list of written instructions to Lieutenant General Nelson A. Miles, Commander of the US Army, concerning US aspirations and policy towards the Hawaiian Islands, Puerto Rico and Cuba.

A few weeks after the Breckenridge Memorandum was issued, on February 15, 1898, at 10 a.m., the battleship Maine *exploded in Havana Bay. Two hundred and sixty sailors, the majority of them black, died in that explosion, while the officers, all white, were safe on shore. This incident was used by the United States as a pretext to intervene in the Spanish-Cuban war on the eve of Cuba's victory over Spain.*

Department of War
Office of the Undersecretary
Washington D.C.
December 24, 1897

Dear Sir,

This department, in accordance with the departments of foreign trade and the navy, feels obligated to complete the instructions on the military organization of the upcoming campaign in the Antilles with certain observations on the political mission that will fall to you as general in charge of our troops. Until now, the annexation of territories to our Republic has been that of vast, sparsely populated regions, and such annexation has always been preceded by our immigrants' peaceful settlement, so the absorption of the existing population has been simple and swift.

In relation to the Hawaiian Islands, the problem is more complex and dangerous, given the diversity of races and the fact that the Japanese interests there are on the same footing as ours. But taking into account their meager population, our flow of immigrants will render those problems illusory.

The Antillean problem has two aspects: one related to the island of Cuba and the other to Puerto Rico; as well, our aspirations and policies differ in each case.

Puerto Rico is a very fertile island, strategically located to the extreme east of the Antilles, and within reach for the nation that possesses it to rule over the most important communications route in the Gulf of Mexico, the day (which will not tarry, thanks to us) the opening is made in the Isthmus of Darien [the Panama Canal]. This acquisition which we must make and preserve will be easy for us, because in my mind they have more to gain than to lose by changing their sovereignty since the interests there are more cosmopolitan than peninsular.

Conquest will only require relatively mild measures. Our occupation of the territory must be carried out with extreme care and respect for all the laws between civilized and Christian nations, only resorting in extreme cases to bombing certain of their strongholds.

In order to avoid conflict, the landing troops will take advantage of uninhabited points on the southern coast. Peace-loving inhabitants will be rigorously respected, as will their properties.

I particularly recommend that you try to gain the sympathy of the colored race with the double objective of first obtaining its support for the annexation plebiscite, and second, furthering the main motive and goal of US expansion in the Antilles, which is to efficiently and rapidly solve our internal race conflict, a conflict which is escalating daily due to the growth of the black population. Given the well-known advantages that exist for them in the western islands, there is no doubt that once these fall into our hands they will be flooded by an overflow of black emigrants.

The island of Cuba, a larger territory, has a greater population density than Puerto Rico, although it is unevenly distributed. This population is made up of whites, blacks, Asians and people who are a mixture of these races. The inhabitants are generally indolent and apathetic. As for their learning, they range from the most refined to the most vulgar and abject. Its people are indifferent to religion, and the majority are therefore immoral and simultaneously they have strong passions and are very sensual. Since they only possess a vague notion of what is right and wrong, the people tend to seek pleasure not through work, but through violence. As a logical consequence of this lack of morality, there is a great disregard for life.

It is obvious that the immediate annexation of these disturbing elements into our own federation in such large numbers would be sheer madness, so before we do that we must clean up the country, even if this means using the methods Divine Providence used on the cities of Sodom and Gomorrah.

We must destroy everything within our cannons' range of fire. We must impose a harsh blockade so that hunger and its constant companion, disease, undermine the peaceful population and decimate the Cuban army. The allied army must be constantly engaged in reconnaissance and vanguard actions so that the Cuban army is irreparably caught between two fronts and is forced to undertake dangerous and desperate measures.

The most convenient base of operations will be Santiago de Cuba and Oriente province, from which it will be possible to verify the slow invasion from Camagüey, occupying as quickly as possible the ports necessary for the refuge of our squadrons in cyclone season. Simultaneously, or rather once these plans are fully in effect, a large army will be sent to Pinar del Río province with the aim of completing the naval blockade of Havana by surrounding it on land; but its real mission will be to prevent the enemy from consolidating its occupation of the interior, dispersing operative columns against the invading army from the east. Given the impregnable character of Havana, it is pointless to expose ourselves to painful losses in attacking it.

The troops in the west will use the same methods as those in the east.

Once the Spanish regular troops are dominated and have withdrawn, there will be a phase of indeterminate duration, of partial pacification in which we will continue to occupy the country militarily, using our bayonets to assist the independent government that it constitutes, albeit informally, while it remains a minority in the country. Fear, on one hand, and its own interests on the other, will oblige the minority to become stronger and balance their forces, making a minority of autonomists and Spaniards who remain in the country.

When this moment arrives, we must create conflicts for the independent government. That government will be faced with these difficulties, in addition to the lack of means to meet our demands and the commitments made to us, war expenses and the need to organize a new country. These difficulties must coincide with the unrest and violence among the aforementioned elements, to whom we must give our backing.

To sum up, our policy must always be to support the weaker against the stronger, until we have obtained the extermination of them both, in order to annex the Pearl of the Antilles.

The probable date of our campaign will be next October [1898], but we should tie up the slightest detail in order to be ready, in case we find ourselves in the need to precipitate events in order to cancel the development of the autonomist movement that could annihilate the separatist movement. Although the greater part of these instructions are based on the different meetings we have held, we would welcome from you any observations that experience and appropriate action might advise as a correction, always, in the meantime, following the agreed upon lines.

Sincerely yours,

J.C. Breckenridge

DOCUMENT 2

THE TREATY OF PARIS (DECEMBER 10,1898)

Her Majesty the Queen Regent of Spain, in the name of her August Son Don Alfonso XIII, and the United States of America, desiring to end the state of war now existing between the two countries, have for that purpose appointed as Plenipotentiaries:

Her Majesty the Queen Regent of Spain,

Don Eugenio Montero Rios, President of the Senate;

Don Buenaventura Abarzuza, Senator of the Kingdom and ex-Minister of the Crown;

Don José de Garnica, Deputy to the Cortes and Associate Justice of the Supreme Court;

Don Wenceslao Ramírez de Villa-Urrutia, Envoy Extraordinary and Minister Plenipotentiary at Brussels; and

Don Rafael Cerero, General of Division;

And the President of the United States,

William R. Day, Cushman K. Davis, William P. Frye, George Gray and Whitelaw Reid, citizens of the United States;

Who, having assembled in Paris, and having exchanged their full powers, which were found to be in due an3d proper form, have, after discussion of the matters before them, agreed upon the following articles:

Article I

Spain relinquishes all claim of sovereignty over and title to Cuba.

And as the island is, upon its evacuation of Spain, to be occupied by the United States, the United States will, so long as such occupation shall last, assume and discharge the obligations that may, under international law, result from the fact of its occupation, for the protection of life and property.

Article II

Spain cedes to the United States the island of Puerto Rico and other islands now under Spanish sovereignty in the West Indies, and the island of Guam in the Marianas or Ladrones.

Article III

Spain cedes to the United States the archipelago known as the Philippine Islands, and comprehending the islands lying within the following lines:

A line running from west to east along or near the 20th parallel of north latitude, and through the middle of the navigable channel of Bachi, from the one hundred and eighteenth (118th) to the one hundred and twenty-seventh (127th) degree meridian of longitude east of Greenwich, thence along the one hundred and twenty-seventh (127th) degree meridian of longitude east of Greenwich to the parallel of four degrees and forty-five minutes (4°45′) north latitude, thence along the parallel of four degrees and forty-five minutes (4°45′) north latitude to its intersection with the meridian of longitude one hundred and nineteen degrees and thirty-five minutes (119°35′) east of Greenwich, thence along the meridian of longitude one hundred and nineteen degrees and thirty-five minutes (119°35′) east of Greenwich to the parallel of latitude seven degrees and forty minutes (7°40′) north, thence along the parallel of latitude seven degrees and forty minutes (7°40′) north to its intersection with the one hundred and sixteenth (116th) degree meridian of longitude east of Greenwich, thence by a direct line to the intersection of the tenth (10th) degree parallel of north latitude with the one hundred and eighteenth (118th) degree meridian of longitude east of Greenwich, and thence along the one hundred and eighteenth (118th) degree meridian of longitude east of Greenwich to the point of beginning.

The United States will pay to Spain the sum of twenty million dollars ($20,000,000), within three months after the exchange of the ratifications of the present treaty.

Article IV

The United States will, for the term of 10 years from the date of the exchange of the ratifications of the present treaty, admit Spanish ships and merchandise to the ports of the Philippine Islands on the same terms as ships and merchandise of the United States.

Article V

The United States will, upon the signature of the present treaty, send back to Spain, at its own cost, the Spanish soldiers taken as prisoners of war on the capture of Manila by the American forces. The arms of the soldiers in question shall be restored to them.

Spain will, upon the exchange of the ratifications of the present treaty, proceed to evacuate the Philippines as well as the island of Guam, on terms similar to those agreed upon by the Commissioners appointed to arrange for the evacuation of Puerto Rico and other islands in the West Indies, under the Protocol of August 12, 1898, which is to continue in force until its provisions are completely executed.

The time within which the evacuation of the Philippine Islands and Guam shall be completed shall be fixed by the two Governments. Stands of colors, uncaptured war vessels, small arms, guns of all calibers, with their carriages and accessories, powder, ammunition, livestock and materials and supplies of all kinds, belonging to the land and naval forces of Spain in the Philippines and Guam, remain the property of Spain. Pieces of heavy ordinance, exclusive of field artillery in the fortifications and coast defences, shall remain in their emplacements for the term of six months, to be reckoned from the exchange of ratifications of the treaty; and the United States may, in the meantime, purchase such material from Spain, if a satisfactory agreement between the two Governments on the subject shall be reached.

Article VI

Spain will, upon the signature of the present treaty, release all prisoners of war and all persons detained or imprisoned for political offenses, in connection with the insurrections in Cuba and the Philippines and the war with the United States.

Reciprocally, the United States will release all persons made prisoners of war by the American forces, and will undertake to obtain the release of all Spanish prisoners in the hands of the insurgents in Cuba and the Philippines.

The Government of the United States will, at its own cost, return to Spain and the Government of Spain will, at its own cost, return to the United States, Cuba, Puerto Rico and the Philippines, according to the situation of their respective homes, prisoners released or caused to be released by them, respectively, under this article.

Article VII

The United States and Spain mutually relinquish all claims for indemnity, national and individual, of every kind, of either Government or of its citizens or subjects, against the other Government, that may have arisen since the beginning of the late insurrection in Cuba and prior to the exchange of ratifications of the present treaty, including all claims for indemnity for the cost of the war.

The United States will adjudicate and settle the claims of its citizens against Spain relinquished in this article.

Article VIII

In conformity with the provisions of Articles I, II and III of this treaty, Spain relinquishes in Cuba and cedes in Puerto Rico and other islands in the West Indies, in the island of Guam, and in the Philippine Archipelago, all the buildings, wharves, barracks, forts, structures, public highways and other immovable property which, in conformity with law, belong to the public domain, and as such belong to the Crown of Spain.

And it is hereby declared that the relinquishment or cession, as the case may be, to which the preceding paragraph refers, cannot in any respect impair the property or rights which by law belong to the peaceful possession of property of all kinds, of provinces, municipalities, public or private establishments, ecclesiastical or civic bodies, or any other associations having legal capacity to acquire and possess property in the aforesaid territories renounced or ceded, or of private individuals of whatsoever nationality such individuals may be.

The aforesaid relinquishment or cession, as the case may be, includes all documents exclusively referring to the sovereignty relinquished or ceded that may exist in the archives of the Peninsula. Where any document in such archives only in part relates to said sovereignty, a copy of such part will be furnished whenever it shall be requested. Like rules shall be reciprocally observed in favor of Spain in respect of documents in the archives of the islands above referred to.

In the aforesaid relinquishment or cession, as the case may be, are also included such rights as the Crown of Spain and its authorities possess in respect of the official archives and records, executive as well as judicial, in the islands above referred to, which relate to said islands or the rights and property of their inhabitants. Such archives and records shall be carefully preserved, and private persons shall, without distinction, have the right to require, in accordance with law, authenticated copies of the contracts, wills, and other instruments forming part of notarial protocols or files, or which may be contained in the executive or judicial archives, be the latter in Spain or in the islands aforesaid.

Article IX

Spanish subjects, natives of the Peninsula residing in the territory over which Spain by the present treaty relinquishes or cedes her sovereignty, may remain in such territory or may remove therefrom, retaining in either event all their rights of property, including the right to sell or dispose of such property or of its proceeds; and they shall also have the right to carry on their industry, commerce and professions, being subject in respect thereof to such laws as are applicable to other foreigners. In case they remain in the territory, they may preserve their allegiance to the Crown of Spain by making, before a court of record, within a year from the date of the exchange of ratifications of this treaty, a declaration of their decision to preserve such allegiance, in default of which declaration, they shall be held to have renounced it and to have adopted the nationality of the territory in which they may reside.

The civil rights and political status of the native inhabitants of the territories hereby ceded to the United States shall be determined by the Congress.

Article X

The inhabitants of the territories over which Spain relinquishes or cedes her sovereignty shall be secured in the free exercise of their religion.

Article XI

The Spaniards residing in the territories over which Spain by this treaty cedes or relinquishes her sovereignty shall be subject in matters civil as well as criminal to the jurisdiction of the courts of the country wherein their reside, pursuant to the ordinary laws governing the same; and they shall have the right to appear before such courts, and to pursue the same course as citizens of the country to which the courts belong.

Article XII

Judicial proceedings pending at the time of the exchange of ratifications of this treaty in the territories over which Spain relinquishes or cedes her sovereignty shall be terminated according to the following rules:

1. Judgements rendered either in civil suits between private individuals, or in criminal matters, before the state mentioned, and with respect to which there is no recourse or right of review under the Spanish law, shall be deemed to be final, and shall be executed in due term by competent authority in the territory within which such judgements should be carried out.

2. Civil suits between private individuals which may on the date mentioned be undetermined, shall be prosecuted to judgement before the court in which they may then be pending or in the court that may be substituted therefor.

3. Criminal actions pending on the date mentioned before the Supreme Court of Spain against citizens of the territory which by this treaty ceases to be Spanish, shall continue under its jurisdiction until final judgement; but such judgement having been rendered, the execution thereof shall be committed to the competent authority of the place in which the case arose.

Article XIII

The rights of property secured by copyrights and patents acquired by Spaniards in the island of Cuba, and in Puerto Rico, the Philippines and other ceded territories, at the time of the exchange of the ratifications of this treaty, shall continue to be respected. Spanish scientific, literary and artistic works, not subversive of public order in the territories in question, shall continue to be admitted free of duty into such territories, for the period of ten years, to be reckoned from the date of the exchange of the ratifications of this treaty.

Article XIV

Spain shall have the power to establish consular offices in the ports and places of the territories the sovereignty over which has been either relinquished or ceded by the present treaty.

Article XV

The Government of each country will, for the term of ten years, accord to the merchant vessels of the other country, the same treatment in respect of all port charges, including entrance and clearance dues, light dues, and tonnage duties, as it accords to its own merchant vessels, not engaged in the coastwise trade.

This article may at any time be terminated on six months notice given by either Government to the other.

Article XVI

It is understood that any obligations assumed in this treaty by the United States with respect to Cuba are limited to the time of its occupancy thereof, but it will, upon the termination of such occupancy, advise any Government established in the island to assume the same obligations.

Article XVII

The present treaty shall be ratified by Her Majesty the Queen Regent of Spain, and by the President of the United States by and with the advice and consent of the Senate thereof; and the ratifications shall be exchanged at Washington within six months from the date hereof, or earlier if possible.

In faith whereof, we, the respective Plenipotentiaries have signed this treaty.

DOCUMENT 3

THE PLATT AMENDMENT (MARCH 2, 1901)

Whereas the Congress of the United States of America by an Act approved March 2, 1901, provided as follows:

That in fulfillment of the declaration contained in the Joint Resolution approved April 20th, 1898, entitled "For the recognition of the independence of the people of Cuba, demanding that the Government of Spain relinquish its authority and government in the island of Cuba, and to withdraw its land and naval reserve forces from Cuba and Cuban waters, and directing the President of the United States to carry these resolutions into effect," the President is hereby authorized to "leave the government and control of the island of Cuba to its people," so soon as a government shall have been established in said island under a constitution which, either as a part thereof or in an ordinance appended thereto, shall define the future relations of the United States with Cuba, substantially as follows:

Article I

That the government of Cuba shall never enter into any treaty or other compact with any foreign power or powers which will impair or tend to impair the independence of Cuba, or in any manner authorize or permit any foreign power or powers to obtain by colonization or, for military or naval purposes or otherwise, lodgement in or control over any portion of said island.

Article II

That said government shall not assume or contract any public debt, to pay the interest upon which, and to make reasonable sinking fund provision for the ultimate discharge of which, ordinary revenues of the island, after defraying the current expenses of government shall be inadequate.

Article III

That the government of Cuba consents that the United States may exercise the right to intervene for the preservation of Cuban independence, the maintenance of a government adequate for the protection of life, property and individual liberty, and for discharging the obligations with respect to Cuba imposed by the Treaty of Paris on the United States, now to be assumed and undertaken by the government of Cuba.

Article IV

That all Acts of the United States in Cuba during its military occupancy thereof are ratified and validated, and all lawful rights acquired thereunder shall be maintained and protected.

Article V

That the government of Cuba will execute and, as far as necessary, extend the plans already devised or other plans to be mutually agreed upon, for the sanitation of the cities of the island, to the end that a recurrence of epidemic and infectious diseases may be prevented, thereby assuring protection to the people and commerce of Cuba, as well as to the commerce of the southern ports of the United States and of the people residing therein.

Article VI

That the Isle of Pines shall be omitted from the proposed constitutional boundaries of Cuba, the title thereto being left to future adjustment by treaty.

Article VII

That to enable the United States to maintain the independence of Cuba, and to protect the people thereof, as well as for its own defense, the government of Cuba will sell or lease to the United States land necessary for coaling or naval stations, at certain specified points, to be agreed upon with the President of the United States.

Article VIII

That by way of further assurance the government of Cuba will embody the foregoing provisions in a permanent treaty with the United States.

DOCUMENT 4

AGREEMENT ON COALING AND NAVAL STATIONS
(FEBRUARY 16/23, 1903)

AGREEMENT:

Between the Republic of Cuba and the United States of America
for the lease (subject to terms to be agreed upon by the two
Governments) to the United States of lands in Cuba for coaling
and naval stations.

The Republic of Cuba and the United States of America, being
desirous to execute fully the provisions of Article VII of the Act
of Congress approved March 2nd, 1901, and of Article VII of the
Appendix to the Constitution of the Republic of Cuba promulgated
on the 20th of May, 1902, which provide:

> That to enable the United States to maintain the independence
> of Cuba, and to protect the people thereof, as well as for its
> own defense, the Government of Cuba will sell or lease to the
> United States land necessary for coaling or naval stations, at
> certain specified points, to be agreed upon with the President
> of the United States.

have reached an agreement to that end, as follows:

Article I

The Republic of Cuba hereby leases to the United States, for the
time required for the purposes of coaling and naval stations, the

following described areas of land and water situated in the Island of Cuba:

1. In Guantánamo (see Hydrographic Office Chart 1857).

From a point on the south coast, 4.37 nautical miles to the eastward of Windward Point Light House, a line running north (true) a distance of 4.25 nautical miles;

From the northern extremity of this line, a line running west (true), a distance of 5.87 nautical miles;

From the western extremity of this last line, a line running southwest (true), 3.31 nautical miles;

From the southwestern extremity of this last line, a line running south (true), to the seacoast.

This lease shall be subject to all the conditions named in Article II of this agreement.

2. In Northwestern Cuba (see Hydrographic Office Chart 2036).

In Bahía Honda (see Hydrographic Office Chart 520b).

All that land included in the peninsula containing Cerro del Morrillo and Punta del Carenero situated to the westward of a line running south (true) from the north coast at a distance of thirteen hundred yards east (true) from the crest of Cerro del Morrillo, and all the adjacent waters touching upon the coast line of the above described peninsula and including the estuary south of Punta del Carenero with the control of the headwaters as necessary for sanitary and other purposes.

And in addition all that piece of land and its adjacent waters on the western side of the entrance to Bahía Honda included between the shore line and a line running north and south (true) to low water marks through a point which is west (true) distant one nautical mile from Pta. del Cayman.

Article II

The grant of the foregoing Article shall include the right to use and occupy the waters adjacent to said areas of land and water, and to improve and deepen the entrances thereto and the anchorages therein, and generally to do any and all things necessary to fit the premises for use as coaling or naval stations only, and for no other purpose.

Vessels engaged in the Cuban trade shall have free passage through the waters included within this grant.

Article III

While on the one hand the United States recognizes the continuance of the ultimate sovereignty of the Republic of Cuba over the above described areas of land and water, on the other hand the Republic of Cuba consents that during the period of the occupation by the United States of said areas under the terms of this agreement the United States shall exercise complete jurisdiction and control over and within said areas with the right to acquire (under conditions to be hereafter agreed upon by the two Governments) for the public purposes of the United States any land or other property therein by purchase or by exercise of eminent domain with full compensation to the owners thereof.

Done in duplicate at Havana, and signed by the President of the Republic of Cuba this the 16th day of February 1903.

(signed) T. Estrada Palma

Signed by the President of the United States on the 23rd day of February, 1903

(signed) Theodore Roosevelt

DOCUMENT 5

COMPLEMENTARY AGREEMENT OF THE FEBRUARY 16/23, 1903 AGREEMENT ON COALING AND NAVAL STATIONS (JULY 2, 1903)

The Republic of Cuba and the United States of America, being desirous to conclude the lease of areas of land and water for the establishment of naval or coaling stations in Guantánamo and Bahía Honda the Republic of Cuba made to the United States by the Agreement of February 16/23, 1903, in fulfillment of the provisions of Article Seven of the Constitutional Appendix of the Republic of Cuba, have appointed their Plenipotentiaries to that end:

The President of the Republic of Cuba, José M. García Montes, Secretary of Finance and acting Secretary of State and Justice:

And the President of the United States of America, Herbert G. Squiers, Envoy Extraordinary and Minister Plenipotentiary in Havana who, after communicating to each other their respective full powers, found to be in due form, have agreed upon the following Articles:

Article I

The United States of America agrees and covenants to pay to the Republic of Cuba the annual sum of two thousand dollars, in gold coin of the United States, as long as the former shall occupy and use said areas of land by virtue of said Agreement.

All private lands and other real property within said areas shall be acquired forthwith by the Republic of Cuba. The United States of America agrees to furnish to the Republic of Cuba the sums necessary for the purchase of said private lands and properties and such sums shall be accepted by the Republic of Cuba as advance payment on account of rental due by virtue of said Agreement.

Article II

The said areas shall be surveyed and their boundaries distinctly marked by permanent fences or inclosures. The expenses of construction and maintenance of such fences or inclosures shall be borne by the United States.

Article III

The United States of America agrees that no person, partnership or corporation shall be permitted to establish or maintain a commercial, industrial or other enterprise within said areas.

Article IV

Fugitives from justice charged with crimes or misdemeanors amenable to Cuban law, taking refuge within said areas, shall be delivered up by the United States authorities on demand by duly authorized Cuban authorities.

On the other hand, the Republic of Cuba agrees that fugitives from justice charged with crimes or misdemeanors amenable to United States law, committed within said areas, taking refuge in Cuba territory, shall on demand, be delivered up to duly authorized United States authorities.

Article V

Materials of all kinds, merchandise, stores and munitions of war imported into said areas, for exclusive use and consumption therein, shall not be subject to payment of customs duties nor any other fees or charges, and the vessels which may carry same shall not be subject to payment of port, tonnage, anchorage or other fees except in case said vessels shall be discharged without the limits of said areas; and said vessels shall not be discharged without the limits of said areas, otherwise than through a regular port of entry of the Republic of Cuba when both cargo and vessel shall be subject to all Cuban Customs laws and regulations and payment of corresponding duties and fees.

It is further agreed that such materials, merchandise, stores and munitions of war shall not be transported from said areas into Cuban territory.

Article VI

Except as provided in the preceding Article vessels entering into or departing from the Bays of Guantánamo and Bahía Honda within the limits of Cuban territory shall be subject exclusively to Cuban laws and authorities, and orders emanating from the latter in all that respects port police, Customs or Health, and authorities of the United States shall place no obstacle in the way of entrance and departure of said vessels except in case of a state of war.

Article VII

The lease shall be ratified and the ratifications shall be exchanged in the City of Washington within seven months from this date.

In witness whereof, We, the respective Plenipotentiaries, have signed this lease and hereunto affixed our Seals.

Done at Havana, in duplicate, in Spanish and English, this 2nd day of July, 1903.

(signed) José M. García Montes

(signed) H.G. Squiers

DOCUMENT 6

TREATY ON THE ISLE OF PINES (MARCH 2, 1904)

The Republic of Cuba and the United States of America, being desirous to give full effect to the sixth Article of the Provision in regard to the relations to exist between Cuba and the United States, contained in the Act of the Congress of the United States of America, approved March 2nd, 1901, which sixth Article aforesaid is included in the Appendix to the Constitution of the Republic of Cuba, promulgated on the 20th day of May, 1902, and provides that "The Island of Pines shall be omitted from the boundaries of Cuba specified in the Constitution, the title of ownership thereof being left to future adjustment by treaty"; have for that purpose appointed as their Plenipotentiaries to conclude a treaty to that end:

The President of the Republic of Cuba, Gonzalo de Quesada, Envoy Extraordinary and Minister Plenipotentiary of Cuba to the United States of America; and

The President of the United States of America, John Hay, Secretary of State of the United States of America;

Who, after communicating to each other their full powers, found in good and due form, have agreed upon the following Articles:

Article I

The United States of America relinquishes in favor of the Republic of Cuba all claim of title to the Island of Pines situated in the Caribbean Sea near the southwestern part of the Island of Cuba, which has been or may be made in virtue of Articles I and II of the Treaty of Peace between the United States and Spain, signed at Paris on the 10th day of December, 1898.

Article II

This relinquishment, on the part of the United States of America, of claim of title to the said Island of Pines, is in consideration of the grants of coaling and naval stations in the Island of Cuba heretofore made to the United States of America by the Republic of Cuba.

Article III

Citizens of the United States of America who, at the time of the exchange of ratifications of this treaty, shall be residing or holding property in the Island of Pines shall suffer no diminution of the rights and privileges which they have acquired prior to the date of exchange of ratifications of this treaty; they may remain there or may remove therefrom, retaining in either event all their rights of property, including the rights to sell or dispose of such property or of its proceeds and they shall also have the right to carry on their industry, commerce and professions being subject in respect thereof to such laws as are applicable to other foreigners.

Article IV

The present treaty shall be ratified by each party in conformity with the respective Constitutions of the two countries, and the ratifications shall be exchanged in the City of Washington as soon as possible.

IN WITNESS WHEREOF, we the respective Plenipotentiaries have signed this treaty and hereunto affixed their seals.

Done at Washington, in duplicate, in Spanish and English, this 2nd day of March 1904.

(Signed) Gonzalo de Quesada (Seal)

(Signed) John Hay (Seal)

DOCUMENT 7

TREATY OF RELATIONS (MAY 29, 1934)

FRANKLIN D. ROOSEVELT,
President of the United States of America.

TO ALL TO WHOM THESE PRESENTS SHALL COME,
GREETING:

KNOW YE, that whereas a Treaty of Relations between the United
States of America and the Republic of Cuba, was concluded and
signed by their respective Plenipotentiaries at Washington on the
29th day of May, 1934, a true copy of which treaty is word for
word as follows:

The United States of America and the Republic of Cuba,
being animated by the desire to fortify the relations of friendship
between the two countries and to modify, with this purpose, the
relations established between them by the Treaty of Relations
signed at Havana, May 22, 1903, have appointed, with this
intention, as their Plenipotentiaries:

The President of the United States of America, Mr. Cordell Hull,
Secretary of State of the United States of America, and Mr. Sumner
Welles, Assistant Secretary of State to the United States of America;
and:

The Provisional President of the Republic of Cuba, Señor Dr. Manuel Márquez Sterling, Ambassador Extraordinary and Plenipotentiary of the Republic of Cuba to the United States of America;

Who, after having communicated to each other their full powers which were found to be in good and due form, have agreed upon the following articles:

Article I

The Treaty of Relations which was concluded between the two contracting parties on May 22, 1903, shall cease to be in force, and is abrogated, from the date on which the present Treaty goes into effect.

Article II

All the acts effected in Cuba by the United States of America during its military occupancy of the island, up to May 20, 1902, the date on which the Republic of Cuba was established, have been ratified and held as valid; and all the rights legally acquired by virtue of those acts shall be maintained and protected.

Article III

Until the two contracting parties agree to the modification of the agreement in regard to the lease to the United States of America of lands in Cuba for coaling and naval stations signed by the President of the Republic of Cuba on February 16, 1903, and by the President of the United States of America on the 23rd day of the same month and year, the stipulations of that agreement with regard to the naval station of Guantánamo shall continue in effect. The supplementary agreement in regard to naval or coaling stations signed between the two Governments on July 2, 1903, also shall continue in effect in the same form and on the same conditions with respect to the naval station at Guantánamo.

So long as the United States of America shall not abandon the said naval station of Guantánamo or the two Governments shall not agree to a modification of its present limits, the station shall continue to have the territorial area that it now has, with the limits that it has on the date of the signature of the present Treaty.

Article IV

If at any time in the future a situation should arise that appears to point to an outbreak of contagious disease in the territory of either of the contracting parties, either of the two Governments shall, for its own protection, and without its act being considered unfriendly, exercise freely and at its discretion the right to suspend communications between those of its ports that it may designate and all or part of the territory of the other party, and for the period that it may consider to be advisable.

Article V

The present Treaty shall be ratified by the contracting parties in accordance with their respective constitutional methods; and shall go into effect on the date of the exchange of their ratifications, which shall take place in the city of Washington as soon as possible.

IN FAITH WHEREOF, the respective Plenipotentiaries have signed the present Treaty and have affixed their seals hereto.

DONE in duplicate, in the English and Spanish languages, at Washington on the 29th day of May, 1934.

(Seal) Cordell Hull
(Seal) Sumner Welles
(Seal) M. Márquez Sterling

AND WHEREAS, the Senate of the United States of America by their resolution of May 31 (Legislative day, Monday, May 28),

1934 (two-thirds of the Senators present concurring therein), did advise and consent to the ratification of the said treaty;

NOW, THEREFORE, be it known that I Franklin D. Roosevelt, President of the United States of America, having seen and considered the said treaty, do hereby, in pursuance of the aforesaid advise and consent of the Senate, ratify and confirm the same and every article and clause thereof.

IN TESTIMONY WHEREOF, I have caused the seal of the United States of America to be hereunto affixed.

DONE at the City of Washington this 5th day of June, in the year of our Lord 1934 and of the Independence of the United States of America the hundred and fifty-eight.

(Seal) Franklin D. Roosevelt
By the President:

(Signed) William Phillips
Acting Secretary of State

DOCUMENT 8

301. MEMORANDUM FROM THE DEPUTY LEGAL ADVISOR (MEEKER) TO SECRETARY OF STATE RUSK (WASHINGTON, FEBRUARY 2, 1962)

On February 8, Rusk sent this memorandum to McGeorge Bundy for the President with a covering memorandum that reads: "I believe the President might be interested in the attached legal comment on our position in Guantánamo. The political aspects are also being studied."

SUBJECT: Guantánamo Base

Problem:

What are the rights and legal position of the United States in the event of a Cuban denunciation of the Guantánamo Base arrangements?

Conclusions

If Cuba were to denounce and repudiate the arrangements by which the United States has a base at Guantánamo, the United States would be on strong ground to assert (1) that the Cuban denunciation and repudiation were ineffective; (2) that we retained our base rights; and (3) that we would be justified in resisting with force any attempt to evict our armed forces from the base. These conclusions stem from the following considerations:

(a) The right of the United States in Guantánamo is more than a right to maintain a base on territory under the sovereignty of Cuba and governed by Cuban law; by international agreement and treaty the United States obtained the lease of a defined area and received from Cuba the right of "complete jurisdiction and control" in that area.

(b) No date was set for the termination of these rights, and the relevant international instruments specify that they are to continue until modified or abrogated by agreement between the United States and Cuba.

Background

In February 1903 the President of Cuba and President Theodore Roosevelt signed an "Agreement for the Lease to the United States of Lands in Cuba for Coaling and Naval Stations." This included a lease covering the Guantánamo base, whose boundaries were described in Article I of the Agreement. Article II stated: "While on the one hand the United States recognizes the continuance of the ultimate sovereignty of the Republic of Cuba over the above described areas of land and water, on the other hand the Republic of Cuba consents that during the period of the occupation by the United States of said areas under the terms of this agreement the United States shall exercise complete jurisdiction and control over and within said areas..." The Agreement contained no terminal date and no provision for termination.

The Treaty of Relations with Cuba which was signed in May 1903 (and ratified the following year) stated in Article VII:

"That to enable the United States to maintain the independence of Cuba, and to protect the people thereof, as well as for its own defense, the Government of Cuba will sell or lease to the United States lands necessary for coaling or naval stations, at certain specified points, to be agreed upon with the President of the United States."

On the basis of the February 1903 Agreement for Lease and the above-quoted Article VII in the 1903 Treaty of Relations, a lease was signed July 2, 1903 and ratified later that year. The lease specified a rental, and contained certain other provisions in pursuance of the February Agreement.

In 1934 a new Treaty of Relations was signed with Cuba in May and brought into force June 9 of that year. The 1934 Treaty expressly abrogated the Treaty of Relations signed May 22, 1903. However, Article III of the 1934 Treaty contained the following provision on Guantánamo:

"Until the two contracting parties agree to the modification or abrogation of the stipulations of the agreement in regard to the lease to the United States of America of lands in Cuba for coaling and naval stations signed by the President of the Republic of Cuba on February 16, 1903, and by the President of the United States of America on the 23rd day of the same month and year, the stipulations of that agreement with regard to the naval station of Guantánamo shall continue in effect. The supplementary agreement in regard to naval and coaling stations signed between the two Governments on July 2, 1903, also shall continue in effect in the same form and on the same conditions with respect to the naval station at Guantánamo. So long as the United States of America shall not abandon the said naval station of Guantánamo or the two Governments shall not agree to a modification of its present limits, the station shall continue to have the territorial area that it now has, with the limits that it has on the date of the signature of the present Treaty."

As to the Isle of Pines, the 1903 Treaty of Relations had provided as follows in Article VI:

"That the Isle of Pines shall be omitted from the proposed constitutional boundaries of Cuba, the title thereto being left to future adjustment by treaty."

In March 1904 the United States and Cuba signed a Treaty by which the United States relinquished in favor of Cuba "all claim of title to the Island of Pines." Article II of this treaty provided:

"This relinquishment, on the part of the United States of America, of claim of title to the said Island of Pines, is in consideration of the grants of coaling and naval stations in the Island of Cuba heretofore made in the United States of America by the Republic of Cuba."

The treaty was ratified and entered into force 21 years later, in March 1925.

Discussion

The United States presence in Guantánamo rests upon international agreements containing no termination date and making no provision for unilateral termination. Our rights subsist "until the two contracting parties agree to the modification or abrogation" of the Guantánamo lease arrangements.

These arrangements differ from the military base agreements concluded in recent years, since the United States is given a right of "complete jurisdiction and control" in a defined base area. The Guantánamo arrangement more nearly resembles the arrangements with Panama concerning the Canal Zone than the military base agreements concluded by the United States with NATO allies and others during the last 12 years. In the case of the Canal Zone, the United States was granted "in perpetuity the use, occupation and control" of the Zone. The grant covered "all the rights, power, and authority within the Zone... which the United States would possess and exercise if it were the sovereign of the territory." Another analogy is Article III of the Treaty of Peace with Japan, under which the United States received "the right to exercise all and any powers of administration, legislation and jurisdiction over the territory and inhabitants" of the Ryukyu Islands, pending the placing of these islands under trusteeship. It has been recognized that Japan retains residual sovereignty.

A declaration by Cuba that it denounced, repudiated, or abrogated the Guantánamo Base arrangements would be legally ineffective. Those arrangements are to continue, according to their terms, until agreed otherwise between the United States and Cuba. An allegation of the doctrine of *rebus sic stantibus* (changed circumstances) as a ground for unilateral termination would not be well founded. Application of the doctrine has never been upheld by an international judicial tribunal. The leading writers on international law state that the doctrine may be applied only by agreement of the parties or through the decision of a tribunal.

Thus, if Cuba should claim that unilateral statements or actions on its part operated to deprive the United States of its Guantánamo base rights, we would be on strong legal ground in refuting this contention, and in using the necessary force to defend the base at Guantánamo and maintain our position there.

The treaty stipulations regarding the Isle of Pines, made in the Treaty of Relations of 1903 and the separate 1904 treaty ratified in 1925, do not affect the status of the Guantánamo Base. The latter treaty merely stated that the transfer of the Isle of Pines was in consideration of the "grants of coaling and naval stations... heretofore made" (i.e., Guantánamo). United States rights in the base were fixed by the terms of those grants and are not affected by any political connection with the transfer of the Isle of Pines.

DOCUMENT 9

NOTE ON THE UNITED STATES NAVAL STATION AT GUANTÁNAMO BAY

This note by UN legal counsel Constantin Stavropoulos was dated November 7, 1962.

I. History

1. The establishment of the United States naval station at Guantánamo Bay appears to have been part of the settlement which resulted in Cuban independence at the beginning of the present century. A Cuban revolt against Spain broke out in 1895, and the United States became embroiled in the struggle against Spain in February 1898. By the Treaty of Paris of 10 December, 1898, Spain relinquished its rights over Cuba. This was followed by three years of United States military occupation until the proclamation of the Cuban Constitution on 20 May 1902. By an Act approved on 2 March, 1901, the United States Congress laid down certain principles defining "the future relations of the United States with Cuba." Article VII thereof provided as follows:

> That to enable the United States to maintain the independence of Cuba, and to protect the people thereof, as well as for its defense, the Government of Cuba will sell or lease to the United States lands necessary for coaling or naval stations at

certain specified points to be agreed upon with the President of the United States.

Other principles limited Cuba's future treaty making powers, its capacity to incur public debts, and conferred on the United States the right to intervene in Cuba in certain circumstances. All the principles embodied in the Act of Congress were included in an annex to the Cuban Constitution. These were also included in a Treaty of Relations between the United States and Cuba, signed in Havana on 22 May, 1903.

2. In order to implement Article VII of the above-mentioned Act of Congress, the United States and Cuba concluded two Agreements in the course of 1903 on the "Lease of Coaling or Naval Stations." The first of these was signed in February 1903. The preamble thereof recites that the United States and Cuba are "desirous to execute fully the provisions of Article VII of the Act of Congress approved March 2nd, 1901, and of Article VII of the Appendix to the Constitution of the Republic of Cuba…" It then proceeds to give the full text of that Article, and states that "to that end" (i.e. implementation of Article VII) the parties have reached an Agreement. Article I of that Agreement lays down that:

> The Republic of Cuba hereby leases to the United States, for the time required for the purposes of coaling and naval stations, the following described areas of land and water situated in the Island of Cuba…

It goes on to define *inter alia* the area of the Guantánamo naval station. Article II defines certain rights of the United States over the land and water adjacent to "the grant" contained in Article I. Article III, which is the last article, reads, in part, as follows:

> While on the one hand the United States recognizes the continuance of the ultimate sovereignty of the Republic of Cuba over the above described areas of land and water, on the other

hand the Republic of Cuba consents that during the period of the occupation by the United States of said areas under the terms of this agreement the United States shall exercise complete jurisdiction and control over and within said areas...

The Agreement contains no provisions either limiting its duration (beyond the qualification in Article I that the lease is "for the time required for the purpose of coaling and naval stations"), or providing for its amendment or denunciation.

3. The second Agreement on the "Lease of Coaling or Naval Stations" was concluded subsequent to the one just described, and came into force upon the exchange of instruments of ratification on 6 October 1903. This Agreement defines certain of the "conditions of lease" referred to in the first Agreement. Article I provides for an annual payment by the United States to Cuba of "two thousand dollars, in gold coin of the United States, as long as the former shall occupy and use said areas of land..." Article II provides for the proper demarcation of the leased areas. Articles III, IV, V, and VI regulate such matters as commercial undertakings in the leased areas; procedures for surrendering fugitives from justice; customs and harbor fees etc. As with the earlier Agreement, no provisions are included regarding duration, amendment or denunciation.

4. The above two Agreements concluded in 1903 appear to provide the present legal basis for the United States claim to the naval station at Guantánamo Bay. They do not seem to have been amended by any other formal arrangements, although, in his Annual Message to the United States Congress in December 1912, President Taft made reference to an understanding whereby the United States had agreed to release certain land at Bahía Honda, also leased in the first Agreement of 1903, in return for an enlargement of the Guantánamo Naval Base.

5. While the Agreements of 1903 on the "Lease of Coaling or Naval Stations" appear to have remained without any major alteration

since they were concluded, some of the other international engagements to which they have a historical connection have been substantially changed. The Treaty of Relations of 22 May, 1903, referred to in paragraph 1 above and embodying the full text of principles of the Act of Congress of 2 March, 1901, was abrogated in 1934, and replaced by a new Treaty which in effect abolished certain of those principles which had limited the treaty making power of Cuba, placed restrictions upon its capacity to contract public debts, and given the United States the right to intervene in Cuba in certain circumstances. The Treaty of Relations of 1934 nonetheless maintained, in its Article III, the principle relating to the leasing of coaling or naval stations in the following terms:

> Until the two contracting parties agree to modification or abrogation of the stipulations of the agreement in regard to the lease to the United States of America of lands in Cuba for coaling and naval stations signed by the President of the Republic of Cuba on February 16, 1903, and by the President of the United States of America on the 23rd day of the same month and year, the stipulations of that agreement with regard to the naval station of Guantánamo shall continue in effect. The supplementary agreement in regard to naval or coaling stations signed between the two Governments on July 2, 1903, also shall continue in effect in the same form, and on the same conditions with respect to the naval station at Guantánamo. So long as the United States of America shall not abandon the said naval station of Guantánamo or the two Governments shall not agree to a modification its present limits, the station shall continue to have the territorial area that it now has, with the limits that it has on the date of the signature of the present Treaty.

6. In paragraph 1 above it was indicated that the principles contained in the Act of Congress of 2 March, 1901, were embodied

in an annex to the Cuban Constitution promulgated in May 1902. A new Constitution was adopted by Cuba in 1940, which does not appear to have embodied any of the principles. The Constitution of 1940 has now been replaced by a new one of 17 February 1959 which likewise does not contain any of the principles.

II. Comments

7. Briefly speaking, it may be surmised that the United States would seek to defend its legal claim to the Guantánamo naval station on the basis of the two Agreements of 1903 described in paragraphs 2 and 3 above and of Article III of the Treaty of Relations of 1934 which reaffirms those Agreements. It could maintain that the Agreements of 1903 make no provision for unilateral denunciation and that the Treaty of 1934 envisages a change in those Agreements only by way of negotiation and agreement between the two parties. Furthermore, it may also point out that the Treaty of 1934 does not provide for unilateral denunciation, that it has not been replaced by any subsequent treaty, and that it therefore also remains in force. The United States would thus be relying upon a fundamental principle of international law, often expressed in the maxim *pacta sunt servanda*, namely that States must abide by their treaty obligations.

8. On the other hand, it may be surmised that Cuba would seek to argue that the Agreements of 1903 belong to a category of "unequal treaties" as they were in fact imposed upon Cuba as one of the conditions for its independence. Furthermore, this argument might continue, even while this in itself would be sufficient to vitiate the Agreements, they could also be considered invalid on the basis of the change of circumstances which has taken place since 1903. The Act of Congress of 2 March, 1901, from which the Agreements derived, advanced *inter alia* as a basis for establishing the naval station the maintenance of the independence of Cuba and the

protection of the people thereof. In present circumstances, it could be argued, there is not only no longer any need for such protection but, on the contrary, by its very existence, given the attitude of the United States towards Cuba, the station constitutes a threat to the independence of Cuba. Finally, Cuba might seek to argue that by seeking to establish what was in fact a perpetual lease of Cuban territory to another State, the Agreements of 1903 were no longer consonant with the present state of international law and the current conceptions of sovereignty and independence. In other words, Cuba would be invoking one of the grounds recognized by many authorities on international law for the dissolution or expiration of treaties, which is expressed in the maxim *rebus sic stantibus*, namely that all treaties are concluded on the implied condition that their validity is conditioned by a continuation of the circumstances which gave rise to them and that a vital change of circumstances renders them invalid.

9. It would be beyond the scope of the present note to seek to evaluate in any detail the respective legal merits of the two positions outlined above. The possible United States position would appear to rest upon one of the fundamental concepts of traditional international law, but it does not perhaps give full weight to the history of the question and the changes which have taken place both in international law and in relations between the United States and Cuba since 1903. The possible Cuban position, on the other hand, might be considered to stress the history of the question and changed conditions at the expense of legal considerations. The doctrine of *rebus sic stantibus*, because it is so easily open to abuse as a means of not fulfilling unwelcome treaty obligations, is confined by most authorities to the narrowest bounds, such as impossibility of performance or the fact that the treaty concerned imperils the existence or vital development of one of the parties. It is also often maintained that this doctrine

does not automatically release a State from its treaty obligations, but entitles it to claim such release from the other party or parties. If the other party or parties refuse to accede to the request—particularly if this is accompanied by an offer to submit the issue to judicial determination—then the requesting State may be justified in declaring it no longer considers itself bound by the treaty. In any event, from the practical point of view and legal considerations apart, for as long as the United States continues to occupy the Guantánamo Naval Base, a peaceful adjustment or settlement can only be reached by negotiation when the atmosphere would be conducive to such a negotiation.

10. A situation somewhat similar to the present one arose in 1947, when Egypt submitted to the Security Council a complaint concerning, *inter alia*, the stationing of United Kingdom troops in Egypt. In the course of the [UN Security] Council consideration of this time the representative of Egypt argued that the Anglo-Egyptian Treaty of 1936, under which United Kingdom troops were stationed in his country, was no longer valid as it had been concluded in special circumstances, namely the impending outbreak of the Second World War, which no longer existed. Furthermore, it had been imposed upon Egypt. He also argued that the maintenance of foreign troops in Egypt was contrary to the sovereign equality of nations and the system of collective security established by the [UN] Charter. Therefore the Treaty of 1936 was inconsistent with the Charter. Under Article 103 of the Charter, the latter's provisions must prevail in cases of conflict with other international obligations. In reply the representative of the United Kingdom stated that the Treaty of 1936 had still a specified number of years to run, that the United Kingdom was prepared at any time to enter into negotiations for its revision, and that Egypt had failed to make out a case in view of its duty to settle disputes in accordance with international law and having

in mind the principle *pacta sunt servanda*. The legal proposition espoused by Egypt appears to have been expressly supported only by the representatives of Poland and of the USSR. The remaining Members of the Council, on the other hand, sought to stress that a solution to the problem should be reached through direct negotiations between Egypt and the United Kingdom. Three resolutions to this effect were introduced into the Council but, apparently because of differences over their wording and Egyptian objection to direct negotiations, none of them succeeded in obtaining the necessary majority. It may be surmised that if Cuba were to bring a complaint to the Council, in the present circumstances, against the maintenance of the United States naval station at Guantánamo Bay similar arguments would be advanced, and the majority of the Council might again propose a negotiated settlement, at best.

Constantin Stavropoulos
November 7, 1962

DOCUMENT 10

STATEMENT BY THE GOVERNMENT OF CUBA TO THE NATIONAL AND INTERNATIONAL COMMUNITY (JANUARY 11, 2002)

The US naval base at Guantánamo is a facility located in an area of 117.6 square kilometers of the national territory of Cuba, occupied since 1903 due to the Agreement on Coaling and Naval Stations signed by the government of the United States of America and the government of Cuba under President Tomás Estrada Palma. At that time, our country was not really independent since an amendment — known as the Platt Amendment — had been passed by the US Congress and signed by President McKinley in March 1901, while our country was under occupation by the US Army after its intervention in the independence war waged by the Cuban people against the Spanish metropolis.

The Platt Amendment, which granted the United States the right to intervene in Cuba, was imposed to the text of our 1901 Constitution as a prerequisite for the withdrawal of the North American troops from the Cuban territory. Following that clause, the aforementioned Agreement on Coaling and Naval Stations was signed on February 1903 in Havana and Washington, respectively. It actually included two areas of our national territory: Bahía Honda and Guantánamo, although a naval base was never established in the former.

In Article II of that Agreement, the right was literally granted to the United States to do "all that is necessary to outfit those places so they can be used exclusively as coaling or naval stations, and for no other purpose."

In addition to that treaty of February 1903, on May 22 that same year a Permanent Treaty of Relations was signed by Cuba and the United States of America using the exact text of the eight clauses contained in the Platt Amendment which were thus turned into articles of said treaty.

Twenty-one years later, on May 29, 1934, in the spirit of the American "Good Neighbor" policy under President Franklin Delano Roosevelt, a new Treaty of Relations was subscribed between the Republic of Cuba and the United States of America that abrogated the previous 1903 treaty, thereby abrogating the Platt Amendment. The new treaty definitely excluded Bahía Honda as a possible base, but it sustained the presence in Guantánamo Naval Base and kept in effect the rules of establishment. As for such rules that remained in force, the Article III of the new treaty literally stated:

> Until the two contracting parties agree to the modification of the agreement in regard to the lease to the United States of America of lands in Cuba for coaling and naval stations signed by the President of the Republic of Cuba on February 16, 1903, and by the President of the United States of America on the 23rd day of the same month and year, the stipulations of that agreement with regard to the naval station of Guantánamo shall continue in effect. The supplementary agreement in regard to coaling and naval stations signed between the two Governments on July 2, 1903 also shall continue in effect in the same form and on the same conditions with respect to the naval station at Guantánamo. So long as the United States of America shall not abandon the said naval station of Guantánamo or the two Governments shall not agree to a modification of its present limits, the station shall continue to have the territorial

area that it now has, with the limits that it has on the date of the signature of the present Treaty.

As evidence of the abusive conditions imposed by that treaty, the above-mentioned supplementary agreement established that the United States would compensate the Republic of Cuba for the leasing of 117.6 square kilometers — that is, 11,760 hectares comprising a large portion of one of the best bays in the country — with the sum of $2,000 annually, presently increased to $4,085 annually — that is, 34.7 cents per hectare — to be paid to Cuba in yearly checks. An elemental sense of dignity and absolute disagreement with what happens in that portion of our national territory has prevented Cuba from cashing those checks which are issued to the Treasurer General of the Republic of Cuba, a position and an institution that ceased to exist a long time ago.

After the victory of the revolution in Cuba, that base was the source of considerable friction between Cuba and the United States. The overwhelming majority of the over 3,000 Cubans who worked there were fired from their jobs and replaced by people from other countries. At present, only 10 Cubans work there.

In the past, shots were often fired from that facility against our territory, and several Cuban soldiers died as a result. Counterrevolutionaries found haven and support over there. Following unilateral decisions by leaders of the US government throughout the revolutionary period in Cuba, tens of thousands of immigrants — Haitians and Cubans who tried to make it to the United States by their own means — were taken to that military base. Throughout more than four decades, that base has been put to multiple uses, none of them contemplated in the agreement that justified its presence in our territory.

But, Cuba could do absolutely nothing to prevent it. On the other hand, for almost half a century propitious conditions have never existed for a calm, legal and diplomatic analysis aimed at the only logical and fair solution to this prolonged, chronic and abnormal situation, that is, the return to our country of that portion of our national territory occupied against the will of our people.

However, a basic principle of Cuba's policy toward this bizarre and potentially dangerous problem between Cuba and the United States, which is decades long, has been to avoid making our claim a major issue, not even an especially important issue, among the multiple and grave differences existing between the two nations. In the Oath of Baraguá pronounced on February 19, 2000, the issue of the Guantánamo base is dealt with in the last point and formulated in the following way: "In due course, since it is not our main objective at this time, although it is our people's right and one that we shall never renounce, the illegally occupied territory of Guantánamo should be returned to Cuba!"

That military enclave is the exact place where North American and Cuban soldiers stand face to face, thus the place where serenity and a sense of responsibility are most required. Although we have always been willing to fight and die in defense of our sovereignty and our rights, the most sacred duty of our people and their leaders has been to preserve the nation from avoidable, unnecessary and bloody wars.

At the same time, this is also the place where it would be easier for people interested in bringing about conflicts between the two countries to undertake plans aimed at attracting aggressive actions against our people in their heroic political, economic and ideological resistance vis-a-vis the enormous power of the United States.

Our country has been particularly conscious of applying there an especially cautious and equable policy. It should be pointed out, however, that even if for decades there was quite a lot of tension in the area of the Guantánamo naval base, there have been changes there in the past few years and now an atmosphere of mutual respect prevails.

In 1994, when a large number of rafters [would-be Cuban

emigrants] sent by the US authorities concentrated there, the situation created determined the need to solve the numerous problems that had been accumulating, which endangered the lives of many. Some people interested in migrating to the United States from our own territory attempted to do so through the base, while not a few tried to leave the US military base and return to our country by crossing minefields. Accidents occurred and often our soldiers had to take major risks to rescue people from the mine-fields. Such actions also required information and cooperation from the personnel stationed at the base. Additionally, there were the heavy rains and swollen rivers in the area that swept away mines and blurred their markings which gave rise to similarly hazardous situations for all.

Such circumstances contributed to an improvement of the atmosphere there and to authorized, albeit minimal, contacts that were indispensable to those in positions of responsibility on both sides of the base area. Consequently, what prevails there today is not what could be described as an atmosphere of hostility or war.

Two new international developments have had a bearing on the situation in that base: the war in Kosovo in 1999 and the war in Afghanistan after the terrorist acts of September 11. In both cases, the United States has played a protagonist role. In the former case there were a large number of Kosovar refugees. The government of the United States of America, in accordance with previous commitments, made the decision to use the military base to shelter a number of these refugees. Such decisions were always made unilaterally; we were never previously asked our view; and, we were never even informed. However, on that occasion, for the first time, we were informed of the decision and the rationale behind it. We then gave a constructive response. Although we were opposed to that war, there was no reason for us to oppose the assistance that the Kosovar refugees might need. We even offered our country's cooperation, if necessary, to provide medical care or any other services that might be required. Ultimately, the refugees were not sent to Guantánamo naval base.

This time the decision has been adopted to bring prisoners of the war in Afghanistan to that military base. As in the past, we were not consulted but a gesture was made in providing ample and detailed information on the steps that would be taken to accommodate the prisoners there and ensure that the security of our people was not in anyway jeopardized. The latest details were given to the Cuban authorities last Monday, January 7, 2002.

The information supplied indicates that there will be a strong reinforcement of the military personnel at the base in charge of taking the necessary measures for the accomplishment of their objectives.

Despite the fact that we hold different positions as to the most efficient way to eradicate terrorism, the difference between Cuba and the United States lies in the method and not in the need to put an end to that scourge—so familiar to our people who have been the victim of terrorism for more than 40 years—the same that last September 11 dealt a repulsive and brutal blow to the US people.

Although the transfer of foreign prisoners of war by the US government to one of its military facilities—located in a portion of our land over which we have no jurisdiction, as we have been deprived of it—does not abide by the provisions that regulated its inception, we shall not set any obstacles to the development of the operation.

Having been advised of the operation and aware of the fact that it demands a considerable movement of personnel and means of air transportation, the Cuban authorities will keep in contact with the personnel at the US naval base to adopt such measures as may be deemed convenient to avoid the risk of accidents that might put in jeopardy the lives of the personnel thus transported.

Despite the major increase of military personnel that such an operation will require, we feel that it does not pose any threat to the national security of our country. Therefore, we will not increase the Cuban personnel or the military means stationed in the area of that facility. Our highly disciplined and qualified personnel suffice to ensure the safety of the population in the region in case of any danger that might originate with the transfer of the foreign prisoners to that base.

Cuba will make every effort to preserve the atmosphere of détente and mutual respect that has prevailed in that area in the past few years. The government of Cuba appreciates the previous information supplied and has taken note with satisfaction of the public statements made by the US authorities in the sense that the prisoners will be accorded an adequate and humane treatment that may be monitored by the International Red Cross. Although the exact number of prisoners that will be concentrated there is not yet known, just like on the occasion of the project to transfer to that place thousands of Kosovar refugees, we are willing to cooperate with the medical services required as well as with sanitation programs in the surrounding areas under our control to keep them clean of vectors and pests. Likewise, we are willing to cooperate in any other useful, constructive and humane way that may arise.

This is the position of Cuba!

Government of the Republic of Cuba,
January 11, 2002

DOCUMENT 11

STATEMENT FROM THE MINISTRY OF FOREIGN AFFAIRS:
CUBA CALLS ON THE UNITED STATES TO STOP THE
TORTURE OF PRISONERS IN GUANTÁNAMO
(JANUARY 19, 2005)

On January 19, 2005, reflecting the indignation of our people at
the atrocities committed on prisoners held at the US naval base
in Guantánamo, the Ministry of Foreign Affairs presented the
US governmental authorities in Havana and Washington with
a diplomatic note denouncing the flagrant violations of human
rights that the said government is daily committing on Cuban territory illegally occupied by the above-mentioned naval base. This
communication called for an immediate end to that inhuman and
criminal conduct.

The note reminds the US government that the atrocities being
committed on the base and the very fact of utilizing that illegally
occupied Cuban territory as a prison, is in violation of numerous
instruments of international law and international humanitarian
law, and moreover, violates the Agreement on Coaling and Naval
Stations signed in February 1903 by the government of the United
States and the Cuban government of that period, in conditions of
inequality and disadvantage for our country, whose independence
was circumscribed via the Platt Agreement.

According to Article II of that agreement, the US government
committed itself to doing everything necessary to ensure that

those locations should be exclusively used as coal or naval stations and for no other objective.

It is also important to recall that when the Cuban authorities were informed — although not consulted — of the US government decision to transfer a group of prisoners from the war in Afghanistan to this US military enclave in Guantánamo, the government of the Republic of Cuba informed national and international opinion in a statement dated January 11, 2002, that "although the transfer of foreign prisoners of war on the part of the government of the United States to one of its military installations located on part of our national territory over which we have been deprived of the right to exercise jurisdiction is not in line with the regulations that gave rise to that installation, we shall not create any obstacles to the development of the operation." Moreover, the statement highlighted that our government had "taken note with satisfaction of public statements from the US authorities in the context of the prisoners receiving adequate and humane treatment."

The dramatic reality of the prisoners detained on the Guantánamo Naval Base, reported by the media to total 550 at the present time, likewise reveals the double standards of the US government in its overworked and manipulative campaign about human rights.

The arbitrary detention of these foreign prisoners without the mediation of a legal trial, as well as the torture and degrading treatment to which they are being subjected, constitute a gross violation of human rights and numerous international treaties and conventions, in particular, the Universal Declaration of Human Rights and the Convention against Torture and other Cruel, Inhuman or Degrading Treatment or Punishment.

With this hypocritical conduct, the government of the United States has demonstrated the falsity of its own public statements and once again has lied to the government of the Republic of

Cuba, to its own people and to the international community by
concealing the horrific acts of torture, cruelty and humiliating and
denigratory treatment of prisoners detained at the Guantánamo
Naval Base, only comparable to the torture inflicted on inmates in
the prison of Abu Ghraib and other penitential establishments in
occupied Iraqi territory.

The Ministry of Foreign Affairs adds its voice to the calls and
demands of the international community that the government
of the United States immediately end these flagrant violations of
prisoners' rights that, moreover, are being committed on illegally
occupied Cuban territory.

Cuba has the total moral right afforded by an irreproachable
history in this context and the right conferred on it to exercise
sovereignty over all parts of Cuban territory to denounce these
abuses and violations that the US government is daily committing
on the detainees held on the Guantánamo Naval Base and to
demand the end of these practices that violate international law.

Havana
January 19, 2005

CHE: A MEMOIR

By Fidel Castro

In this unique political memoir, Fidel Castro writes with great candor and emotion about a historic revolutionary partnership that changed the face of Cuba and Latin America. Fidel creates a vivid portrait of Che Guevara—the man, the revolutionary, and the intellectual—revealing much about his own inimitable determination and character.

This fascinating memoir includes Fidel's speech on the return of Che's remains to Cuba 30 years after his assassination in Bolivia in 1967, and provides a frank assessment of the Bolivian mission.

ISBN 978-1-920888-25-1 (paper)

"For me, it has always been hard to accept the idea that Che is dead. I dream of him often, that I have spoken to him, that he is alive." —**Fidel Castro**

CHE GUEVARA READER
Writings on Politics and Revolution

The bestselling and most comprehensive anthology of Che Guevara's writings.

Recognized as one of *Time* magazine's "icons of the 20th century," Che Guevara became a legend in his own time and has now reemerged as a symbol for a new generation of political activists. Far more than a guerrilla strategist, Che Guevara made a profound and lasting contribution to revolutionary theory and Marxist humanism as demonstrated in this perennial bestseller.

The *Che Guevara Reader* is divided into four sections: the Cuban revolutionary war (1956-59), the years in government (1959-65); Che's writings on the major international struggles of the 1960s and his vision for Latin America; and a fascinating selection of personal letters.

This book includes a comprehensive chronology of Che's life, an index, and many of his classic works, such as "Socialism and Man in Cuba" and his call to create "Two, Three, Many Vietnams," as well as some previously unpublished writings.

ISBN 978-1-876175-69-6 (paper)

CUBAN REVOLUTION READER
A Documentary History of Fidel Castro's Revolution
Edited by Julio García Luis

The Cuban revolution was one of the defining moments of the 20th century, its influence reaching far beyond the shores of the tiny Caribbean island.

This book documents the turbulent 50-year history of Fidel Castro's revolution, from the euphoria of the early years to near economic collapse in the 1990s, and finally the Cuban leader's decision to step down in 2008.

In his introduction, Julio García Luis, offers a critical examination of Cuba's decades-long relationship with the Soviet Union and the epilogue considers the prospects for the revolution without Fidel Castro.

Including a comprehensive chronology and index, this is an essential resource for scholars and others.

ISBN 978-1-920888-89-3 (paper)

OBAMA AND THE EMPIRE

By Fidel Castro

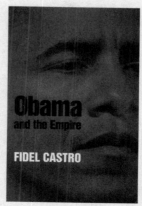

On January 20, 2009, Barack Obama became the 11th president of the United States to confront the reality of the Cuban revolution.

Here, Fidel Castro, one of the chief protagonists of the Cold War and Washington's traditional foe, casts a critical eye over the significance of President Obama's election and his performance during his first term of office.

Since retiring from public life due to ill-health in 2006, the Cuban leader has continued to make characteristically forthright comments on world events in his regularly published "Reflections."

In this book Fidel Castro considers whether Cuba-US relations are finally heading in a new direction. He also discusses a wide range of critical political issues including the global financial crisis, climate change and the environmental crisis, Washington's orientation to Latin America, and the continued US occupation of the Guantánamo naval base. He also challenges the Obama administration's decision to retain Cuba on the list of nations supporting international terrorism.

ISBN 978-0-9804292-6-8 (paper)

FIDEL CASTRO READER

A comprehensive selection of one of the 20th century's most influential political figures and one of history's greatest orators, Fidel Castro.

Opening with Fidel's famous courtroom defense speech following the 1953 attack on the Moncada garrison, this anthology includes more than five decades of Fidel's outstanding oratory, right up to his recent reflections on the future of the Cuban revolution "post-Fidel."

With an extensive chronology on the Cuban revolution, a comprehensive index and 24 pages of photos, this is an essential resource for scholars, researchers and general readers.

ISBN 978-1-920888-88-6 (paper)

"Fidel's devotion to the word is almost magical."
—Gabriel García Márquez

"Fidel is the leader of one of the smallest countries in the world, but he has helped to shape the destinies of millions of people across the globe." **— Angela Davis**

"Fidel Castro is a man of the masses... The Cuban revolution has been a source of inspiration to all freedom-loving people."
—Nelson Mandela

oceanpress
e-mail info@oceanbooks.com.au
www.oceanbooks.com.au